ROB **CARRICK'S** GUIDE

ROB CARRICK'S GUIDE TO WHAT'S

GOOD
BAD AND
DOWNRIGHT AWFUL
IN CANADIAN INVESTMENTS TODAY

DOUBLEDAY CANADA

Doubleday Canada and colophon are registered trademarks.

LIBRARY AND ARCHIVES CANADA CATALOGUING IN PUBLICATION

Carrick, Rob, 1962–

Rob Carrick's guide to what's good, bad and downright awful in Canadian investments today.

ISBN: 978-0-385-66745-6

1. Investments—2. Finance, personal—I. Title

HG5421.C385 2009   332.6   C2009–903965–6

Printed and bound in the USA

Published in Canada by Doubleday Canada,
a division of Random House of Canada Limited

Visit Random House of Canada Limited's website: *www.randomhouse.ca*

10   9   8   7   6   5   4   3   2   1

To my Mom, who got me started in the word business
a long time ago with her love of books

CONTENTS

INTRODUCTION

YOU MAY HAVE NOTICED HOW POLITE, respectful (and, um, boring) most investing books are. There are some good volumes out there on how to invest intelligently, but they so rarely provide the pointed, opinionated direction that people crave at a time when financial information is flying at them from all directions—from word of mouth, newspapers, magazines, books, TV, radio, websites and blogs.

When I'm about to make a major purchase or financial commitment, I want strong opinions from experts. Tell me what works—and, just as importantly, what doesn't. I believe I'm intelligent enough to filter the information to suit my own needs, and I'm pretty sure the same applies to you. That's why the book you're holding is probably the most opinionated, straight-to-the-point investing book you're ever going to read.

Opinions—like there's not enough of *those* in the world already. So why do the ones in this book matter? Let me answer by supplying my qualifications. I worked as a business and economics reporter for close to a decade on both Bay Street and Parliament Hill. I'm a graduate of the Canadian Securities

Course (a preliminary course of study for investment industry people). And for more than ten years I've written the Personal Finance column for *The Globe and Mail,* Canada's national newspaper. I have seen the best and the worst of the investment business over that time and, in my interactions with investing professionals and everyday people, I've discovered a lot of things. Good and bad mutual funds, steadfast dividend stocks, big distortions fostered by the investment industry, indispensable investing newsletters. In this book, I name names and take no prisoners.

After the financial turmoil that flared up in 2008, reliable investing guidance has never been more important. One small benefit of all the market carnage is that it gave me an opportunity to observe the investment industry at a time of maximum stress. My findings in this area are sprinkled throughout the book.

Usability is the key for a book like this, so you'll find the material presented in a list format that allows for cover-to-cover reading, random browsing or cherry-picking. There are lists for people who invest for themselves and for those who use an adviser, and there are lists for beginners as well as intermediate and established investors. No matter how much you know as an investor, there's always something new to learn and brush up on.

This book is designed as a sequel to *How to Pay Less and Keep More for Yourself: The Essential Consumer Guide to Canadian Banking and Investing,* a straight-talk primer on getting the best deals in banking and investing. Reading that book will make you an educated consumer of financial products who can comfortably go nose to nose with bankers, investment advisers and other financial types. Reading this one will take you a step further by providing a road map to what's good, bad and downright awful in Canadian investments today.

One final note before we get rolling. This book was written amid the financial market crisis and recession that hit in the second half of 2008 and was in full swing in the first half of 2009. Naturally, this traumatic development looms large in what follows.

ONE

GETTING YOU OFF
TO A GOOD START

RULE ONE OF BEING A ROOKIE INVESTOR IS THAT you will make mistakes. Rule Two is that some of your mistakes will cost you money. Rule Three is to either get good advice or educate yourself so that you minimize the damage associated with Rules One and Two. To help you in this regard, let's look at some matters of importance to both new and experienced investors.

FOUR EXAMPLES OF INVESTMENT INDUSTRY PROPAGANDA
THAT YOU CAN'T TAKE AT FACE VALUE

The investment industry is forever casting itself in its marketing efforts as a wise and friendly helper that just wants to make you wealthy. Actually, banks, brokerages, fund companies and other financial firms want to make themselves rich, first and foremost. With this end in mind, financial companies spew out all kinds of self-serving chatter designed to make you receptive to the kinds of products and services they sell. Here are some of the most common—well, let's politely call them exaggerations:

1. We are looking out for the best interests of investors.

In any serious profession, there is an ethic of putting the client first. And then there's the business of providing financial advice. While there are many highly ethical people in the financial sector, I feel comfortable saying that the prime directive for many advisers and investment firms is to sell products to generate fees and commissions, not to do right by clients.

Financial companies aren't out to foist their products on you and head for the hills. They want to have a nice relationship with you, based on the concept of them providing a good product that benefits you financially. But, again, the main objective for many is to sell and let everything else take care of itself (or not).

The problem for investors is that they see financial advisers as being on the same level as other professionals like doctors, lawyers and accountants, where there are demanding requirements to entry, strict ethical codes of conduct and organizations that vigorously enforce standards of behaviour. The financial advisory profession is moving in that direction and some advisers are already there. Generally, though, it's prudent to assume until proven otherwise that the person discussing your financial situation with you is primarily interested in making money by selling you products.

2. You need advice to invest properly.

For many people, this is fact. They need advice because they lack the knowledge or time required to make sound investing decisions for themselves. If this is you, be sure to read Chapter Six, where we look at ways to find an adviser and manage your relationship with one. Don't buy the financial industry's nonsense about investing being hazardous to untrained civilians, however. In fact, there's no reason you can't be a successful do-it-yourself investor if you care to learn the basics before you start out. I can tell you from my experience in talking to *Globe and Mail* readers that there are people of all ages and backgrounds who are investing shrewdly and effectively on their own. Most seem to really enjoy it, by the way.

A second point about the financial industry's insistence that you need advice: there's a lot of self-interest involved here. Simply put, advisers are the sales force through which investments end up in the RRSPs, RESPs, tax-free savings accounts and regular investment accounts of everyday people. Ideally, advisers do in fact provide advice in areas such as building a sound retirement fund, minimizing taxes, avoiding debt and estate planning. But many of them—too many, unfortunately—are mainly interested in generating revenue through commissions and fees that come from selling products. For these advisers, advice is a hollow term that puts a gloss on their function as sellers of product.

Note that being a self-directed investor doesn't mean you have to work in a vacuum. There are plenty of sources of help and ideas—books (you're holding one right now), websites, blogs, magazines, newsletters, television and radio programming. You'll find more on this in Chapter Seven.

3. We know what we're doing.
Need I bother to elaborate on this point after the financial market implosion that began in 2008? Lehman Brothers, a 158-year-old Wall Street legend, went bankrupt. Merrill Lynch, an investment dealer with roots going back to 1914 and a peren-

nially high ranking on the *Fortune* 500, became so damaged that it had to be bought by Bank of America. Innumerable hedge funds failed. Widely owned mutual funds lost 40 or 50 per cent of their value. The investing world loves to project a macho aura of extreme competence, but the truth is that a significant number of people either don't know what they're doing or are borderline competent at best.

I would not like you to get the idea here that all, or even most, investment people are dangerous to your financial health. Rather, I hope you'll get over any preconceptions you may have that professional investing people are automatically reliable experts who are qualified for, and deserving of, the job of managing your money for you. Two words of advice: always verify. Ask for references when seeking an investment adviser (Chapter Six has lots more on this theme); check the track record of a mutual fund manager; demand copious documentation when considering investment products that offer something new or make claims that seem to defy the normal rules of investing.

We need to be clear about something when assessing investing professionals. They do make honest mistakes; they are not perfect. Neither are you or I, so we have no right to complain. All we have a right to ask is that the people managing our money are smart and experienced enough to keep mistakes to a reasonable level, both in number and scope.

4. Performance, not fees, is what matters with mutual funds.

People in the investment industry who are mainly concerned with selling products often harp on the idea that fees are immaterial and that bottom-line returns are all that matter. In a simplistic way, this makes sense. If you're making higher returns than most other funds, then why quibble about a fee that's higher than normal?

Here's why. Over the long term, low fees are one of the key contributors to above-average performance. The cost of owning a mutual fund is deducted from its gross returns (reported returns are always net of fees). So the lower the fee, the more there is left over for a fund's clients. When you consider that most funds tend to deliver average returns over the long term, fees can be a key differentiator in terms of ultimate returns for investors. Low fees do not guarantee good returns, but they are a foundation.

I should point out here that it's not just me saying so. The people at the independent mutual fund research firm Morningstar Canada use fees as a key criterion in assembling their list of funds that qualify as analyst favourites. "For anyone who regularly reads our fund analyst reports, we may sound like a bit of a broken record on the fee issue," the firm says on its website at Morningstar.ca. "But the bottom line is, the fees are the one component of a mutual fund's makeup that you can be certain will detract from performance, and many funds simply charge too much." Well put.

QuickSurvey: The Perils of Focusing on Performance When Buying Mutual Funds. Here's how some of one year's top Canadian equity funds performed in the next twelve months.

Fund	2007 Return	2007 Quartile	2008 Return	2008 Quartile
Imaxx Cdn Equity Growth	23.6	1	−40.3	4
IA Clarington Cdn Leaders	17.8	1	−23.5	1
Ethical Canadian Stock	16.7	1	−33.3	2
Desjardins Environment	15.1	1	−32.3	2
Fidelity Cdn Large Cap B	14	1	−29.7	1
Manulife Cdn Core	13.3	1	−41.4	4
Fidelity Cdn Disciplined Eq.	13.2	1	−35.7	3
Investors Cdn Growth A	12.3	1	-53.3	4

Lesson: Relying on recent performance is a pure gamble. You may get another year of pack-leading returns or you may hit bottom.

Note: Quartiles divide funds in a category into four groups according to their returns, with first quartile being the elite and fourth quartile the bottom-feeders.

SEVEN DUMB ROOKIE MISTAKES INVESTORS MAKE AND HOW TO AVOID THEM

Investing is not something you plunge right into and learn on the fly like, say, gardening or cooking. The price of an investing mistake can be a major setback to your retirement savings or a reduction in the amount of money you have available to pay for your kids' post-secondary education. Study these common errors and resolve to learn enough before you start investing in order to avoid them.

1. Buying Hot Stocks and Mutual Funds

First, a confession. The media, of which I am a part, promote this type of foolish investing by making a big deal about the hottest funds and stocks of the moment. These performance numbers are nothing more than trivia. But lots of investors interpret them almost like the standings for professional sports leagues—the guys at the top must be the best.

This may be true. Or maybe the top funds of the moment are actually chronic mediocrities that just happen to be riding one of those periodic hot streaks that even the lamest funds stumble into periodically. These hot streaks are fleeting and usually give way to a period of flat or weak performance that brings the fund back down to the middle of the pack. To buy in after a rally, then, is to buy at the peak and set yourself up for a decline. Mutual funds are properly chosen by applying a variety of criteria, including past performance. But the emphasis has to be on long-term performance, with a secondary level of attention directed to what's happened recently.

Stocks are a bit different here because it often pays to buy the shares of a company riding a wave. This is called momentum investing, and it's best left to managers or individuals who are savvy enough to, first, spot stocks with sustained upward potential and, second, cut their losses if they choose incorrectly.

2. Not Diversifying

Here's the basic idea behind diversification: you own a bunch of different things—stocks or equity funds of various types, bonds and cash—so that a decline in any one type of asset doesn't bring your whole portfolio down. Also, diversification helps increase the odds that there will always be something in your portfolio that is working particularly well.

The reason why many investors ignore diversification or pursue it half-heartedly is that it's such a buzz-kill. The markets are soaring? Then why park money in bonds or cash, especially in these days of low interest rates? It's tempting to downplay diversification in a roaring bull market, and it's profitable, too—until the market falls and rolls back your gains, of course. Bonds and cash are lifeboats in a bad stock market—make sure your portfolio has them. I should hardly even need to make this point after the disasters of 2008 and early 2009.

If you're wondering about the right mix, try the online asset allocation calculators offered by most discount brokers, The general concept behind these tools is to use your age, risk tolerance and other factors to come up with a breakdown of how much of your portfolio should be in the major asset classes. Note: Suggested asset mixes vary, sometimes widely. Go with what feels comfortable, but remember there are risks in being both too aggressive and too conservative.

3. Buying Things You Don't Understand

Investors do this all the time, and things often work out fine. In a fast-rising stock market, it may not matter much what you buy because everything's going up. Eventually, though, ignorance gets dangerous.

Income trusts are a perfect example. Trusts gained huge popularity in the mid-2000s because they paid out cash every month or quarter while also holding out rich potential for share-price increases as well. Many investors, seniors among them, embraced trusts as a source of income on the assumption that the cash payments were utterly reliable and that the share-price increases were a slam dunk.

Both assumptions proved false. Many trusts were built on second-rate businesses that ran into trouble and had to cut or suspend their cash payments. Then, the entire trust market was staggered when the federal government announced a new tax that will apply to these securities starting in 2011. Many trusts plunged in price and had yet to recover all of their losses two years later. Very few people anticipated the new trust tax, but the smart ones limited their exposure so that the damage to their portfolios was limited and manageable. Other investment products that too many people bought over the years without understanding how they work or their risk profiles: principal-protected notes, science and technology funds and labour-sponsored venture capital funds.

4. Selling Too Soon or Too Late

Knowing when to sell is one of the hardest calls to make in investing. It's not the mission of this book to be a tutorial on stock trading, but it is worth looking at two common mistakes in this area. One is selling too soon. Imagine you buy a stock, and it goes down. If you're like some skittish investors, you sell and wonder what you did wrong. The answer might well be nothing. Good stocks go down sometimes and experienced investors know enough to be cool about it. Don't buy a stock unless you have a solid rationale. Return to this line of reasoning to bolster your resolve if the stock goes down without any catastrophic news announcements.

Selling too late is another blunder. If there's one thing you take away from this tiny slice of the book, let it be an understanding of the necessity of deciding how much of a loss you're willing to tolerate in a fund or stock that you own, especially something you've bought as a speculative investment. The example of Nortel Networks shows how futile it can be to hold onto a fast-falling stock in hopes that it will rebound, but it's far from the only example. Not too long ago, the Vancouver-based portfolio manager Adrian Mastracci told me that he was still encountering new clients with flotsam and jetsam in their accounts that dated back to the technology boom that began the 2000s.

5. Buying High and Selling Low

Admit it—when the stock markets tanked in 2008, there were moments when you lost all hope that a rebound would ever occur. Markets have always bounced back from down periods due to depressions, recessions, wars and various other calamities, but this doesn't reassure people. Somehow, they imagine, this time will be different. Folks, when it comes to the stock markets, this time is *never* different. Stocks go up, and they go down. Sometimes, these moves are slow and steady, and other times they're sudden and violent. In the end, though, you get maybe 6 to 8 per cent a year on average over the long term, including dividends. It's that simple.

Every mutual fund company and adviser in creation has tried to get this message across to investors, but it doesn't often take. That's why mutual fund industry statistics unfailingly show investors gorging on stocks after a good run-up in prices has already occurred and then bailing out after a down spell. The right approach is to judiciously take profits after a market rally, and to gradually buy back in when markets plunge. Want to keep things on a simpler plane? Find the right mix of stocks and bonds for your portfolio and stick to it through good and bad times.

6. Thinking GICs Are Risk-Free

The risk of losing your money with guaranteed investment certificates is nil, provided you stick within the limits set out by the Canada Deposit Insurance Corporation and don't put more than $100,000 into GICs at any one financial institution. But that's far from the only risk investors must consider.

There's also the risk of not generating enough investment income to meet your financial goals if you're in the accumulating phase of your financial life, or to meet your income needs if you're retired and living off what your portfolio generates. We have lived in an era of low interest rates, which has meant that building a portfolio of GICs alone is a risky proposition. How do you cut this risk? An easy way is to add conservative, dividend-paying blue-chip stocks. Well-chosen dividend stocks will gradually increase the amount of money they pay over time, thereby increasing the yield on your initial investment. Even during the recent recession, some blue-chip companies were still able to increase their dividends (several cut theirs, mind you). GICs are a dead end—they pay what they pay, and that's it.

7. Mistaking Luck in Stock Trading for Skill

The gods of stock trading are both mischievous and cruel. Often—surprisingly often, actually—they allow rookie investors to do very well on their first trade or two. Maybe it's a routine purchase of a bank stock, or a carefully chosen junior oil and gas company. The rookie buys, and the stock rises enough to delude him or her into thinking, "Hey, I'm a natural."

The word that usually applies here is lucky. This becomes apparent after subsequent trades that don't work out. The investor may then start making even riskier trades in hopes of a big score that makes up for the losses. Eventually, the ledger ends up deep in the red.

Learning stock trading is a bit like taking up a sport in a serious way. You prepare yourself by observing, asking questions and reading up, and then you swing into action on the understanding that there's a learning curve requiring some upfront blundering around. Stock trading is a skill you have to develop by study and practice.

FOUR HARSH INVESTING REALITIES THAT INVESTORS —AMAZINGLY—DON'T ALWAYS GRASP

It's sometimes said that investing is all about the interplay of fear and greed. That's a really cynical take, and a silly simplification. And yet, it may help explain why investors sometimes seem so divorced from market realities like these.

1. Bad times on the stock market are just around the corner.

Okay, after the horror that began in 2008, this is blatantly obvious to every sentient human with a television, radio, newspaper subscription or internet access. As you may recall, the entire global financial system, not just the stock markets, seemed at one point to be collapsing. But while the extent of the market decline was stunning—we need a word here that's more extreme than shocking—the fact that the market fell in 2008 was hardly surprising.

In fact, the Canadian market had turned in five straight years ranging from good to great between 2003 through 2007. Anyone who was unprepared for a decline of some sort in 2008 wasn't paying attention to what was going on. It's often estimated that the stock market will generate, on average, returns of something like 6 to 7 per cent over the long term. If you see annual market returns getting way ahead of this over a period of years, as happened in the 2003–07 time frame, then expect a pullback.

The reason why investors often don't see market downturns coming is that they get used to positive returns and figure they'll continue indefinitely. A smarter approach is to assume the good times will end, suddenly and painfully, and to prepare by having a diversified, high-quality portfolio. Keep a down market in mind when things look good, and look ahead to a rising in market when things look bad.

2. There's no such thing as a safe stock.

There was a time when bank stocks were considered to be quite safe, largely because they went up consistently. Then came the sub-prime mortgage disaster in the United States in 2007. Banks in both the United States and, to a much lesser extent, Canada, were exposed and investors recoiled. Net result: bank stocks were annihilated. Early in 2009, even the comparatively solid Royal Bank of Canada had seen its shares post a cumulative five-year loss of 15 per cent.

What happened to bank stocks is an extreme example of an important point of investing: every stock has its kryptonite. Utility and pipeline companies are thought of as safe widows-and-orphans stocks, but they can fall if interest rates surge. Energy and mining stocks will be huge performers when commodity prices rise, and just the opposite when prices plunge. Food companies are a super way to ride out a bear market, but in boom times they're susceptible to difficulties relating to the competitiveness of the retailing environment.

Remember, there are a few different layers of risk when looking at stocks. There's the macroeconomic risk, as in a recession. Then there's sector-specific risk and company-specific risk. We're talking in this latter example about the potential for a hapless CEO to blow up his company, maybe through a bad merger or acquisition.

There's no question that some stocks are safer—that is, they present less risk of losing money—than others. But *all* stocks are potential money losers. Never forget that when investing in the market directly, or through mutual funds.

3. You need at least a five-year commitment to invest in the stock market, but it sometimes takes ten years or even longer.

I just checked the twenty-year compound average annual return for the S&P/TSX composite index and the magic number was 6.95 per cent. That sounds about right. Most of what I've read over the years suggests that you can expect average annual returns in this zone from investing in the stock market. What investors fail to understand is that this does not mean 6 to 8 per cent *every* year. Rather, it could mean something like annual returns over a five-year span of 5 per cent, 15 per cent, minus-14 per cent, 9 per cent and 20 per cent. These annual returns, of course, average out to 7 per cent.

Now, let's say you bailed on the market after the third year, following the 14-per-cent decline. You made good money in the first two years, but lost enough in the third to reduce your average annual three-year return to just 2 per cent. Hold on a few more years, though, and a rallying market would bring you back up to an average 7 per cent. The point here is that the market is inherently unreliable and inconsistent. You need to stick with it to make money.

Do you really need to stick with it for ten years or more to make money? Let's answer this question by looking at the ten-year average annual return for global equity funds at the time this book was being written. The sorry number was minus-2.9 per cent. Looking back fifteen years, the average return for the global fund category was 1.2 per cent. Over the previous twenty years, it was 3.7 per cent. These numbers aren't definitive—global funds had long been dreadful for a variety of reasons, and a big rebound seemed possible. But they do give you an idea of how much patience can be needed in a worst-case situation if you want to get a decent return out of an investment in stocks.

4. If you buy a stock at $10 and it rises to $20, then falls to $15, you haven't lost $5.

It's funny how some people measure their investment returns. Instead of looking at where they started and comparing it to where they are in the present, they instead fixate on the high-water mark for their holdings. A $10 stock doubles to $20 and then falls back to $15 in a year? To me, that's a pretty cool 50-per-cent profit. Yet some investors would see it as a disappointment—even as a loss of 25 per cent ($20 to $15).

The stock market rarely moves in a straight line for very long. Stocks go up and down, and you can deal with this in two ways. One is to buy great stocks and funds and hold for years so that your money benefits from long-term market growth. Another is to trade actively so that profits are locked in through disciplined selling. Either way, you have to understand that your success is measured in terms of where you started and where you are now. The ups and downs in between are just scenery along the way.

THREE GOOD, QUICK AND EASY WAYS TO GET STARTED
AS A YOUNG INVESTOR

You want to start investing, but you lack both the knowledge to jump in and the time to learn. No sweat—here are a few ways to sensibly get your money working for you in short order.

1. Start an account with an investment adviser who works with your family or has been recommended by someone else.

Using an adviser is the ideal approach for someone who knows zip about investing, other than the fact that it's good to start young. The difficulty is in finding an adviser. We'll look at the adviser-client relationship in detail in Chapter Six, but the issue in this particular case is that advisers don't generally like to work with people who have tiny accounts. The reason: small accounts mean small revenues for the adviser in the form of fees and commissions.

The way around this is to find an adviser who is already doing business, and doing it well, with someone you know and trust. This individual would go to the adviser and say, "I know of a young person with great prospects who is just starting out in the workforce and needs some financial guidance. Would you help out?" The answer is most often going to be yes. For one thing, the adviser will presumably want to keep the existing client happy by accepting the referral. Secondly, referrals are a gift to advisers, most of whom are always thinking about how to expand their client lists.

Ideally, a young person would set up an account, probably an RRSP, with the adviser and start making regular contributions. Over a period of years, the account would grow into something substantial enough to keep the adviser interested and properly compensated.

2. Head to your bank.

A perennial topic of lively debate in the investing industry is whether the banks are a force for good or ill. By way of answering this question in a politically neutral way, let me say that some bank investing products are quite good. Prominent among them are dividend mutual funds, which hold the shares of the kind of big blue-chip companies that form a country's economic foundation.

Pretty well every mutual fund company has a dividend fund, but for some reason, the banks are the best at running them. So whatever bank you deal with, you should feel reasonably safe in walking in and asking to set up a regular contribution plan where money goes out of your bank account and into a dividend fund. Over a decade, you should expect to see your money grow by anywhere from 5 to 10 per cent annually on average, depending on market conditions. Past experience suggests strongly that the average dividend fund will outperform both the average Canadian equity fund and the average Canadian equity focused fund.

One thing to be aware of with dividend funds is that they tend to have extensive holdings in the financial sector, which as we all know got whacked in the 2007–08 period. Bank stocks have done very well over the long term for investors, but they are most decidedly not immune to serious declines from time to time. Dividend funds won't be immune, either.

To balance your bank-centred investment plan, consider adding a global equity fund and a bond fund or ladder of GICs. The ladder concept means dividing your money earmarked for GICs into five chunks that get invested in terms of one through five years. When a GIC matures, it gets rolled over into a new five-year term. Young investors could easily use a mix of 75 per cent dividend funds and 25 per cent GICs.

Starting to invest at a young age is smart, and so is learning to deal with banks. So be sure to ask for an interest rate bonus on any GICs you buy. Half a percentage point is good, but a quarter of a point is better than nothing.

QuickSurvey: Eight Dividend Funds from the Banks and Credit Unions

Fund	MER (%)	Minimum Inv.	10-year Return (%)*	2008 Loss (%)
RBC Cdn Dividend	1.7	$500	7.2	−27
BMO Dividend	1.71	$500	7.8	−26.3
TD Dividend Income	1.92	$100	5.8	−28.8
TD Dividend Growth	1.92	$100	7.2	−29.9
Scotia Cdn Dividend	1.64	$500	6.7	−27.4
National Bank Dividend	1.71	$500	4.9	−19.8
CIBC Dividend Growth	1.92	$500	5.1	−29.1
Ethical Cdn Dividend	2.59	$500	N/A	−27.2
Category Average	2.32		5.0	−26.4

*to December 31, 2008

3. Use an ETF wrap product.

You'll find lots of information in Chapter Three on exchange-traded funds, or ETFs, which are basically index-tracking investment funds that trade like a stock. ETFs started out well more than a decade ago as a way for investors to capture the returns of the most popular stock and bond indexes. Then, in the mid-2000s, they suddenly became trendy. Dozens of cute ETF concepts hit the market, and it's now possible to write them off as being pretty much useless for mainstream investors because of their high degree of specialization. But a few of the new ETF innovations make good sense. For example, ETF wraps, which aim to provide investors with a completely balanced portfolio in a single security.

The iShares and Claymore ETF families in Canada each have a selection of wrap ETFs. Let's take a quick look at the iShares Conservative Core Portfolio Builder Fund, which trades on the Toronto Stock Exchange under the symbol XCR. This ETF is designed for someone who wants the safety of having close to two-thirds of his or her portfolio invested in bonds, with the rest in stocks, commodities, real estate investment trusts and other sectors chosen to enhance returns. iShares, the company behind this ETF, has designed it using the same thinking that goes into the structuring of big pension funds. Over time, the mix of investments is continually rebalanced so that you don't find yourself with more or less exposure to a sector than you expected.

The mutual fund industry offers hundreds of wrap products like this. Most are duds as a result of their high fees. ETF wraps are low-fee leaders for this product category, which is another reason why they're a good choice for young investors who want to put some money to work in an expeditious way.

QuickSurvey: ETF Wraps, or How to Build a Sound Portfolio with a Single Purchase

Fund	Ticker (TSX)	MER (%)
Claymore Balanced Income CorePortfolio ETF	CBD	0.69
Claymore Balanced Growth CorePortfolio ETF	CBN	0.83
iShares Growth Core Portfolio Builder Fund	XGR	0.6
iShares Conservative Core Portfolio Builder Fund	XCR	0.6

TWO

MUTUAL FUNDS

THERE'S ROUGHLY $550 BILLION INVESTED in mutual funds
in Canada, which tells you that an awful lot of people have their
financial aspirations riding on them. That's fine, because funds .
can be a smart way for everyday people to invest. Funds give you
access to top money managers, they're convenient to buy and sell
and they can produce very good results when you choose wisely.
This section of the book is aimed at helping you do just that.

FIVE BITS OF FUND JARGON YOU NEED TO KNOW

I know how opaque most financial jargon is to investors, which is
why I've selected five key examples from the fund world to explain
here. This stuff is vital if you want to get the most value out of your
fund investments.

1. Management Expense Ratio (MER)
In simple terms, the MER tells you how much it costs to own
a mutual fund. It's preferable to have a low MER than a high

one when selecting funds.

Here's how the MER works. First, almost all the fees associated with running a fund are gathered together, including management and administrative fees. Next, these fees are compared to the total assets in the fund. What you end up with is a ratio showing you the percentage of the fund's assets that are eaten up by fees every year. Of course, those assets aren't just sitting there. They're invested in stocks, bonds and other stuff and hopefully earning a return that offsets the fees charged by the fund. Want to know how much a fund needs to make to break even? Just look at the MER. If it's 2.5 per cent, then a gain of 2.5 per cent is needed to get to the break-even point.

One of the most common fund questions I get from investors is, Do fund returns reflect the impact of the MER or not? The answer is yes. Fund companies publish net returns in virtually all cases. Put another way, fund companies take their cut before investors get paid.

MERs are not closely guarded secrets. You can get fee information on fund company websites, in fund company brochures and from websites like Globeinvestor.com and Morningstar.ca. Still, many investors are, by and large, clueless about the cost of owning funds. It's so easy—just check the MER.

I said earlier that the MER includes *almost all* the fees associated with a mutual fund. Curious about what isn't included? Mainly, trading costs—the brokerage commissions a fund pays for buying and selling securities. These trading costs can add as much as one percentage point, perhaps even more, to a fund's total cost, depending on how much trading a fund manager does. You can find hard information on the cost of trading in a mutual fund's semi-annual management report on fund performance. Look for the trading expense ratio, or TER, which expresses trading costs as a percentage of fund assets. Add the MER to the TER and you've got the total cost of owning a fund.

QuickSurvey1: The Cost of Owning a Big Dividend Fund (TD Dividend Growth)

MER: 1.92%

TER: 0.02%

Total cost of owning this fund for the period to June 30, 2008: 1.94%

QuickSurvey2: The Cost of Owning a Big Canadian-Focused Equity Fund (Dynamic Power Canadian Growth)

MER: 2.34%

TER: 0.36%

Total cost of owning this fund for the period to December 31, 2008: 2.70%

2. Trailing Commission

Also known as trailer fees, or just trailers. Ever wonder how investment advisers who sell mutual funds get paid? No, you say, you didn't? You're not alone—a lot of investors are sold funds by advisers without having a clear picture of how the adviser is compensated for the transaction and subsequent service on your account.

Now that you've read the preceding section on management expense ratios, you know all about the big package of fees that eat into a fund's returns. A major component of those fees is the trailing commission. If you own an equity fund with an MER of 2.25 per cent, it would be typical for one percentage point to be accounted for by trailers. The trailer is paid by the fund company directly to the adviser, who shares it with his or her firm. Let's hope you're getting great service from your adviser, because he or she is getting paid well through trailers, regardless of how your account is doing.

Permit me to vent on an especially galling matter connected to trailing commissions, which is that discount brokers collect trailers in the same way as advisers do. Discount brokers, of course, provide no advice. They simply take orders to buy and sell securities. They do little or nothing to warrant getting a full trailing commission, but only two discount brokers have done anything to recognize this. One is RBC Direct Investing, which sells a special class of RBC's own family of funds that has a much-reduced MER. The idea behind these Series D funds is that investors who make their own decisions should pay less for funds.

The other broker is a small firm called Questrade, which offers a service called Mutual Fund Maximizer where you pay $29.95 per month and in return get all your trailer fees rebated back to you. You need to hold at least $36,000 or so in funds to make this economical.

QuickSurvey: A Typical Fund Company's Trailing Commissions for Funds Sold with an Upfront Sales Charge

Fund Type	Trailer
Equity Funds	1%
Balanced Funds	1%
Bond Funds	0.50%
Money Market Funds	0.25%

3. Deferred Sales Charge (DSC)

There was a time when a large majority of the fund purchases in this country were made with a deferred sales charge, which is to say these funds were sold with no upfront commission at all for investors. Instead, these investors put themselves in a position of having to pay a redemption fee—a deferred sales charge—if they cashed out of their funds within the first six or seven years after buying.

The DSC was invented as a way of helping investors circumvent huge upfront sales commissions that were a big turnoff. The problem with DSCs is that they're like financial handcuffs. If you want to sell a fund, whether because of terrible performance or your own personal financial need, you could well have to pay fees of up to 5 or 6 per cent of your investment.

Today, an ever-decreasing percentage of fund sales are made with a DSC, but some investment advisers still actively promote them. The reason is that a fund company will pay an adviser more initially for selling a DSC fund than for selling funds with an upfront sales commission. Selling funds with upfront commissions can be more lucrative over the long term for advisers (because the trailing commissions are higher). But if an adviser needs income right now, he or she will prefer the DSC and accept lower trailers over the long term.

QuickSurvey: A Typical Fund Company's DSC Schedule

Period after Purchase	Redemption Charge Rate
First year	5.5%
Second year	5.0%
Third year	5.0%
Fourth year	4.0%
Fifth year	4.0%
Sixth year	3.0%
Seventh year	2.0%
Thereafter	Nil

4. Zero Load

Interviewing a new financial adviser from whom you expect to buy mutual funds? One of the first questions to ask is whether he or she sells mutual funds with a zero load. A zero-load fund is one where the upfront sales commission has been set at zero or, in other words, waived entirely. Thus there's no commission to pay when buying these funds, and there's no deferred sales charge to worry about if you want to sell later on.

Zero-load advisers have been growing in number, but they remain in the minority. Often, zero-load advisers are well-seasoned professionals who have large books of business and can afford to live off the trailing commissions they get from the funds they've sold over the years. Young advisers may also sell on a zero-load basis as a way of attracting new clients who might be turned off by upfront sales commissions or deferred sales charges.

Don't mistake zero-load funds for no-load funds, which are entirely different. No-load funds are sold by banks and small,

independent fund companies, and investors can always purchase them with no upfront commissions or deferred sales
charges. Zero-load funds, you'll remember, are essentially funds
with an upfront sales commission that has been waived at an
adviser's discretion.

5. Benchmark

This is a term you'll come across in all aspects of investing, not
just in the fund realm. A benchmark is a reference point that
allows investors to correctly judge the performance of a fund
or portfolio of stocks. Typically, benchmarks are widely recognized stock and bond indexes.

Maybe you own a Canadian equity fund and you're becom-
ing more and more convinced it's a complete washout. You
keep reading about how the stock markets are soaring, but your
fund barely moves. How can you accurately judge your fund?
Find the appropriate benchmark and compare returns over
various time frames. For a broadly based Canadian equity fund
with virtually all of its assets in Canada, the S&P/TSX composite is the correct benchmark (even better is the S&P/TSX
composite total return index, which includes dividends). For
U.S. equity funds focusing on big blue-chips, use the S&P 500
stock index. For global equity funds, use the MSCI World
Index. For international equity funds, use the MSCI Europe
Australasia Far East (EAFE) Index. The fund profiles available
on Globeinvestor.com handily provide all the benchmark data
you need to get the lowdown on the funds you own.

Don't give up on your fund because it has lagged on the
market over a year or so. A much better way to use benchmarks

is to compare them to your fund's returns over a period of five or ten years. Any fund at all can have a bad year. What matters is how it compares to the benchmark over longer periods.

THREE EXAMPLES OF FUND INDUSTRY SHENANIGANS

I've been covering the mutual fund industry for more than a decade and here are a few of its practices that really bug me. They should bug you, too.

1. Making a Big Deal about Management Fees

To me, nothing undermines the credibility of a fund company quicker than seeing it publicize the management fees charged by its funds. It's a way of preying on investor ignorance, and the most diplomatic word to describe it is *sneaky*.

Earlier in this chapter, you read about how a mutual fund's MER—the standard reference for understanding how much a fund costs to own—is a bundling together of management fees and administrative fees. Put another way, MERs include the cost of paying managers who run a fund as well as the costs of keeping the fund running—like record-keeping and accounting.

You may now have grasped the idea that management fees are nothing but a component of the total cost of owning mutual funds. In quoting management fees in its marketing material, then, a mutual fund company is giving you only a partial view of what it costs to own its products. Why do fund companies do this? My cynical view is that it's to fool people.

After all, the term *management fee* can easily be mistaken for management expense ratio. Publicize management fees all by themselves, and maybe some people will be fooled into thinking your funds are cheaper to own than they actually are. Frankly, there's absolutely no reason at all for a fund to publicize its management fees, other than in its prospectus. If you see a fund company flogging its management fees in an ad or piece of marketing bumf, then alarm bells should go off.

2. Blowing Smoke about Bad Investing Results

A few years ago, securities regulators did something useful for small investors in requiring fund companies to create regular updates on how their funds were doing. The idea was for these semi-annual management reports on fund performance to describe the results the fund had delivered, and offer some explanation.

Sizing up the quality of these reports in mid-2008, the Ontario Securities Commission delivered a two-word message to the fund industry: Do better. This admonition was well deserved. In a few examples I uncovered, fund companies completely avoided any direct reference to significant losses and instead prattled on in a business-as-usual manner.

Look, too much is sometimes made of a stumble by a fund or fund manager. Mistakes happen, but they're ideally offset and then some by good decisions. Fund companies don't like to admit their errors, though. They'd rather pretend everything's just fine, even when it's plainly not. Here's the ideal template for a fund company explaining a bad patch: "Here's what happened, here's why and here's what we're doing about it." Clients deserve this kind of frankness.

3. Creating Gazillions of Versions of the Same Funds

Many years ago, it was typical for a fund company to offer a mutual fund with a separate version that was priced in U.S. dollars. Then came multiple segregated fund versions, which come with varying types of guarantees about getting your principal back after a set period of time. Then came capital-class versions, which enable investors with non-registered accounts to move between funds in a family without triggering capital gains. Then came systematic-withdrawal versions, which enable investors to remove a set percentage of their investment each year as a way of generating income. Then came currency-hedged versions, which proliferated in the U.S. and global fund categories to insulate returns against moves in the Canadian dollar.

Mutual funds are products, and, of course, product innovation and development are inevitable and, indeed, desirable. But the fund industry has taken this beyond all common sense. By creating so many different types and classes of fund, the industry has laden itself with high administrative costs and created a plague of what we'll call product pollution. Variety is great, but there's too much of it in fundland.

SIX CRUMMY MUTUAL FUNDS THAT MAKE THE INDUSTRY LOOK BAD

The underreported scandal of the mutual fund industry is that there are billions of dollars sitting in sub-par funds that are reliable fee generators for the companies that offer them and nothing more. Here are some examples. Note: What follows is a snapshot of crummy funds at a moment in time. Every dog has its day, which means that any one of these funds could be doing well at the moment you're reading this. Past results are not a definitive indicator of future returns, but you can't ignore them, either.

1. AIC Global Advantage, AIC American Advantage

The AIC Advantage Fund was, at one time, a performance leader among Canadian mutual funds thanks to a timely emphasis on financial stocks. The massacre of this sector between 2007 and 2009 hurt this fund mightily, but we can write this off as a somewhat predictable outcome for a fund heavily (and, defensibly) tilted toward a single sector. What's hard to accept is the fact that AIC created U.S. and global spin-offs of this fund that were also slammed in the global financial crisis. Note: Both these funds were laggards before the market crashed. On the bright side, they were certainly candidates for investors who wanted to buy low in the financial sector in 2009.

2. CIBC Canadian Equity

A Canadian equity fund with a ten-year compound average annual return of 1.7 per cent? What's the point of that? A Canadian money market fund would have made you 2.7 per cent over the ten years to December 31, 2008, with virtually no risk. There's plenty of risk with this fund—in 2008 it lost almost 38 per cent, about five percentage points more than the S&P/TSX composite index. Ouch.

3. Dynamic Money Market

Impressively consistent in one regard—it regularly underperforms the average Canadian money market fund by a small amount. Why would that be? Look no further than the 1.30-per cent management expense ratio (that was the MER of record at the time this was written), which compared to a category average of 1.03 per cent. You won't find a much better example of how paying more for a fund leaves you with less.

4. Fidelity Global

Fidelity is the world's largest fund company, and it's a classy outfit that, I think, tries to do right by its customers. This fund's a dog, though. It's consistently below average, so there are no excuses to be made from the fact that global funds in general were a sinkhole through much of the 2000 decade. In 2008, for example, its loss of 36.1 per cent was about five percentage points worse than the average. Over the previous ten years, it was a couple of points worse than average. From a blue-chip firm like Fidelity, you expect better.

5. Templeton Canadian Stock

The Templeton fund family's edge is global investing, notably through its flagship Templeton Growth Fund. This Canadian equity fund is a complete dud, though. It did modestly better than the S&P/TSX composite index in the treacherous market conditions of 2008, but its longer-term numbers underperform both the index and the category average with dismal consistency. Don Reed, president of Franklin Templeton Investments, took over the fund in June 2008, so take a look to see how things have gone lately.

6. Trimark Discovery

Trimark is among the most conscientious companies in the fund business, and has a respectable stable of funds. And then there's Trimark Discovery, an attempt to cash in on the technology boom of the 1990s. Look at the long- and short-term numbers and it quickly becomes apparent that, apart from a few years in the late 1990s, this fund has struggled. (Trimark seems to have agreed. In Summer '09 this fund was merged into another Trimark fund.)

THREE LOW-PROFILE FUND COMPANIES
YOU SHOULD KNOW ABOUT

Big fund companies have big profiles in most cases because they have big bucks to throw around on marketing that keeps their visibility high. But there are other strata in the fund industry occupied by companies that aren't as well known. These companies are worth following. They're often run by serious investing people who are too focused on running money for pension funds, endowments and wealthy individuals to worry much about scrounging up customers for the mutual funds they also offer. Also, low-profile companies tend to have low fees in many cases. Note: Expect minimum upfront investment requirements of $5,000 to $10,000.

1. Mawer Investment Management

Mawer is that rarity in the mutual fund industry, a company that does everything well, whether it be Canadian equity, U.S. and international equity, balanced or bond funds. The most popular fund in the family is Mawer World Investment, which is notable because firms like Mawer often do Canadian equity funds very well but make a mess out of global and U.S. equities. Mawer World Investment, an international equity fund (everywhere but North America), has been a perennial overachiever.

Interested in balanced funds? Canadian investors are crazy about them, but too few of them know about two of the best: Mawer Canadian Diversified Investment and Mawer Canadian Balanced RSP. Both offer everything investors want in a balanced fund, which means consistent returns coupled with a containment of risk. What could just be the company's best fund, a small-capitalization offering called Mawer New Canada, was at press time capped for new and existing investors. However, there's a nearly identical fund run by the same manager available through the BMO Guardian family called BMO Guardian Enterprise Mutual.

Mawer was founded in the early 1970s by Chuck Mawer, a one-time stockbroker. The firm focused on looking after money for individuals with high net worths, as well as pension funds and the like, and it established a family of investment funds for their use. Today, Mawer has been subcontracted by not only BMO Guardian, but also financial services giant Manulife Financial to run funds. The two distinguishing features of Mawer funds: very low fees and very consistent performance.

More info: mawer.com.

2. Beutel Goodman

Just for laughs during the dark days of the stock market crash of 2008, I would periodically cruise the list of top-performing mutual funds, such as they were. A fund company name I saw several times while running the numbers was Beutel Goodman.

Most investors have never heard of Beutel because its specialty is managing money for company pension plans, private foundations, endowments and individuals with high net worths. Mutual funds are a sideline, a sort of brand extension of the investing work the company does for its institutional clients.

The Beutel style of money management is conservative, which in practical terms means you'll miss the highest highs of a bull market but be spared the worst predations of a bear market. Beutel Goodman Canadian Equity is a prime example. It was a top-tier performer in the bear market years of 2001 and 2002 and something of a laggard in the bull market of mid-decade. Then, in the wretched markets of 2008, it again reasserted itself as a top performer (read more about this fund later in this chapter).

Other good products in the Beutel Goodman family include a low-fee bond fund that is a perennial leader in the Canadian fixed-income category, a good low-fee money market fund and a solid balanced fund. Investors in these funds rarely get to brag about killer returns, but they're compensated by not having to worry much about killer losses. The minimum investment when starting up an account with this firm is $10,000.

More info: beutel-can.com

3. Steadyhand Investment Funds

The president of this newer firm is Tom Bradley, former head honcho of money manager Phillips, Hager & North, which is now part of RBC Asset Management. There are two reasons why Bradley's involvement matters, one of them being PH&N's reputation as a fund company that put investors first when it was under his guidance. The other is Bradley's iconoclastic persona. Anyone this blunt about the fund industry's shortcomings simply has to deliver the goods or run the risk of losing all credibility.

Here's an example from a blog written by Bradley on the Steadyhand website. The posting was a tongue-in-cheek list of honest comments he'd like to see from fund company executives, including: "I want to hear a marketing executive say: 'This fund has an excellent 10-year record, but we just changed the fund manager last week. We suggest you wait to buy.' Or see a firm run an ad featuring their worst five funds over the past three years with the caption: 'Among our 80 funds, this is where the opportunity lies.' Or see them waive the deferred sales commission (DSC) on a fund because: 'In good conscience, we can't charge any more for the pain this fund has caused.'"

Steadyhand is an independent, low-fee fund outfit that sells directly to investors, although you should be able to buy its products through at least some discount brokers and investment advisers. The lineup is fairly small at five funds, but they're all you need to build a portfolio. Don't bother looking for celebrity managers here. Steadyhand has contracted out the management of each of its funds to what it considers to be a roster of the best money managers around. You haven't heard of any of them, most likely, but Bradley has staked his reputation on them. That's saying something.

More info: steadyhand.com

FIVE BIG, FAT MUTUAL FUND INDUSTRY RIP-OFFS

Let's be clear about something: mutual funds are a fine way for the masses to get the benefit of investing in stocks, bonds and other instruments. But if you're not an educated customer, you can easily find yourself in products that primarily make money for the financial industry, rather than individual investors. Here are some traps to look out for.

1. Almost All Money Market Funds

Canadians lo-o-o-ve money market funds, as evidenced by the fact that there was a staggering $70 billion or so sitting in these funds as this book was being written. Sure, money market funds are comparatively safe (though not impervious to loss or guaranteed in any way), and they're conveniently offered by almost every fund company. But they're also one of the most expensive products in the fund universe.

The fees for money market funds average 1.03 per cent, which is not bad on the face of it. By comparison, the average management expense ratio for Canadian equity funds is 2.42 per cent. But if you examine money market fund MERs as a percentage of their average long-term returns, you get a much uglier picture. The average annual return for money market funds for the five years leading up to the writing of this book was 2.3 per cent, which is in large part due to low interest rates. If you're paying

1.03 per cent to make 2.3 per cent, you're being exploited.

There are three types of money market funds out there, only one of which deserves your business. But let's start with the other two. One is the type of money market fund offered by big fund companies. As a rule, these funds are expensive and offered only so as to provide a complete, fully rounded fund lineup. The other avoidable type of money market fund is offered by the big bank fund families. These are the most popular money market funds by far, but they're also too expensive.

Note: The banks all have "premium" low-fee money market funds available to clients with large amounts to invest, say $100,000 to $1 million. If you have the money, these funds are worth a look.

The third class of money market fund, the one you should be looking at, is offered by a few small, low-profile fund companies that are characterized by their low fees and by the fact that their main line of business is running money for pension funds and rich people as opposed to mutual funds. Some names to consider: Beutel Goodman, Leith Wheeler, Mawer Investment Management, McLean Budden and Phillips, Hager & North (a division of Royal Bank of Canada's fund family).

The drawback with these fund families is that they require minimum investments of at least $5,000 to $10,000. If that's prohibitive, then look for the lowest-fee alternative and use it until your account gets large enough that you have that minimum $5,000.

2. Most Bond Funds

Bond funds are a good idea ruined by high fees. You want bonds in your portfolio, right? How else are you going to be able to psychologically withstand the damage done to your portfolio during a grinding bear market. Bonds add stability plus income, and that's a good offset to the volatility of stocks. Now, let's get practical about bonds.

If you don't have a brokerage account, or if your investment adviser isn't licensed to sell stocks and bonds, then bond mutual funds are an obvious answer. With one purchase of a bond fund, you've exposed your portfolio to a collection of bonds that is far more diversified than you could assemble yourself. The problem is that the fee you'll most likely pay for this aggregation of bonds is, on average, laughably high.

As I wrote this book, Globeinvestor.com showed that the average bond fund management expense ratio was 1.65 per cent. Compare that to a concurrent five-year Government of Canada bond yield of 1.7 per cent and a ten-year yield of 2.7 per cent. Now, let's say your bond fund manager adds some corporate bonds to take advantage of their higher yields, and let's also say he's an adept trader who can squeeze some extra returns out of the fund by buying and selling bonds occasionally. Maybe all of this gets your gross return from the portfolio to 3 per cent. Now, apply the average MER of 1.65 per cent. What you're left with in terms of a net, after-fee return is 1.35 per cent.

The big non-bank fund families are the worst for over-charging on bond funds. My theory is that these firms are not especially interested in bond funds because they don't gener-ate as much revenue as equity funds but feel they have to offer them so as to have a well-rounded selection to offer investors and advisers. If you're dumb enough to buy these funds, you get what you deserve. The better move is to look at bond funds from low-fee fund families and, failing that, from bank fund families. Keep your fees down with bond funds and you'll unquestionably reap the benefits through higher returns.

3. Many Balanced Funds

For naked exploitation of unwitting investors, balanced funds have few peers. It's not that balanced funds are, more than anything else, a triumph of packaging and convenience, though they most certainly are. Rather, it's the fact that many of them are outrageously pricey to own.

A prime example is one of the biggest balanced funds in Canada, the RBC Balanced Fund. The management expense ratio here was 2.25 per cent at press time, which is much too high. Here's my thinking: RBC Balanced is what's called a "Canadian neutral balanced" fund, which means it holds stocks and bonds in roughly equal proportions. You could pretty much duplicate this fund by splitting your money between RBC Canadian Equity and RBC Bond, two very popular funds in their own right. RBC Canadian Equity's MER is 1.96 per cent, which isn't too bad at all for its category. RBC Bond's fee is 1.2 per cent, which is okay. Average the MERs for these two funds and you get 1.6 per cent. That's what the MER for RBC Balanced should be.

All right, let's say RBC is justified in adding a bit to the fee for going to the trouble of juggling stocks and bonds in the same fund—that's nonsense, but let's say it, anyway. Even if you padded the MER by another quarter of a percentage point, you still end up way below the fund's actual 2.25 per cent. Why is this fund so expensive, then? Because investors will pay it.

RBC is actually one of the most solid citizens in fundland when it comes to keeping fees reasonable. But it has fallen down on its balanced fund, and it's not alone. Lots of other companies are charging too much for a product that includes a heavy quotient of bonds, which are much less labour intensive to manage than stocks.

4. Bank Index Funds

Make no mistake, I'm a big fan of index investing. Indexing means your returns are based on what a specific stock or bond index makes, minus fees. Indexing stands in contrast to what's known as active management, where a fund manager selects what he or she figures are the best stocks to own. Over any given time frame, you'll find that many, maybe a majority, of actively managed funds don't match the return of their benchmark stock indexes.

Why? Not necessarily because the managers are useless (though quite a few are), but often because of the fees charged by these funds. If a fund has a management expense ratio of 2.5 per cent, it has to earn 2.5 per cent just for the investors to break even. Remember, fees are taken off the top.

This brings us to index funds. They do, in fact, have lower fees, which means the companies offering them are taking less off the top. What's not to like, then? It's that even with their reduced fees, index funds still charge too much. Typically, a bank index fund might charge 0.75 to 1 per cent in fees. If you use exchange-traded funds (ETFs) instead of index funds, you can get those fees down as low as 0.09 to 0.17 per cent.

ETFs—Chapter Three has lots of information on them—do the exact same thing as index funds: they deliver the return of a specific index, minus fees. The difference is that they're listed on stock exchanges and trade like any old stock. Of course, you'll need a brokerage account to invest in ETFs. The benefits, however, include lower fees than pretty much any other kind of fund and, thus, the potential for higher returns.

One exception to this diatribe against bank index funds is the e-Series from TD Asset Management. Read on for more info.

5. Fund Wraps

Wrap programs are an exercise in packaging and marketing more than anything else. Wraps are bundles of mutual funds that have been assembled for various types of investors—conservative, aggressive, people seeking income and so on. The idea of wraps is to eliminate the daunting job of selecting individual mutual funds to suit an investor's needs. Instead, you buy the wrap corresponding to your profile and Bob's your uncle.

Some wraps are okay investments, and yet I think it's safe to say that investors can avoid them entirely and never regret it for a moment. The reason is that wraps are built primarily to generate fees for fund companies and investment firms. You can see this in the way fund firms will bundle their own products together—the good alongside the mediocre and the pitifully weak—and pass off the whole works as a thoughtfully assembled portfolio in a box. You can also see it in the way some wraps are composed of funds from a variety of companies, but with fee surcharges that require you to pay more than if you were to buy all the component funds separately.

Raise the issue of fees with companies offering wraps and you'll get a blast of nonsense about all the inherent benefits of investing this way. Automatic rebalancing of your holdings to make sure everything's in the right proportion (your adviser should be doing this for you automatically, anyway); professionally designed portfolios (many are laughably slapdash and contain too many funds in a kind of overdiversification); and, special account reports (some of these aren't bad, to be fair).

Wraps have been one of the hottest mutual fund products over the past couple of years, and the reasons are important to note because they have little to do with what's right for clients. Wraps cause investors to give all their business to a single fund company rather than parcelling it out to various firms. And, wraps offer something to the individual or adviser who wants to take the easy way out of portfolio-building. Avoid.

FIVE GREAT DEALS IN FUNDLAND

Low fees provide a firm foundation that helps these funds deliver consistently good returns for those investors smart enough to own them.

1. Phillips, Hager & North Bond

PH&N Bond of Vancouver was once the king of independent fund companies, but then it got snapped up by Royal Bank of Canada. RBC committed to keeping PH&N Bond's family of funds much as they were, which is why this gem of a bond fund is included here.

The first thing to note about this fund is that it's run by PH&N's crack team of bond fund managers. These guys play in a higher league than most of their peers, a point you can see in PH&N Bond's perennial ranking as a top-tier Canadian bond fund. Even great managers slip to the bottom tier once in a while, but these guys have brought new meaning to the word consistency.

A major reason for this is the fund's ultra-low management expense ratio of 0.59 per cent (we're talking about the D version here), compared to the average of about 1.65 per cent for the Canadian fixed income fund category. Put another way, PH&N's managers have to clear a hurdle of 0.59 per cent before they start making money for unitholders, while their average peers have to generate 1.65 per cent before clients start to benefit.

If you're interested in this fund, the D version is available directly from PH&N and through some discount brokers. There's also a C version, but it has a somewhat higher MER to cover the payment of trailing commissions to advisers and discount brokers. The D version pays no trailers, and that's a big reason why it's so blessedly cheap to own. The minimum investment is $5,000, compared to $1,000 for the C series.

2. The TD e-Series of Index Funds

TD's e-Series is *the* answer for people who want to be index investors but lack the brokerage account and a large enough portfolio to use exchange-traded funds, or ETFs. An ETF is like a stock that gives you the same return as any one of dozens of Canadian, U.S. and global stock indexes. The benefit of indexing is that you often get higher returns than from mutual funds run by people who choose their own stocks rather than mimicking an index.

If you want to invest in ETFs, you of course need a brokerage account. Remember, you're buying index funds that trade like stocks. The sticking point here for some investors is that they usually have to pay a brokerage commission every time they want to add to their ETF holdings. If you're on a monthly contribution plan for your RRSP account, this can get pricey, even when you're paying as little as $5 to $30 per trade using a discount broker's online trading service.

This brings us to TD's e-Series of funds, which are no-load index funds available only over the Internet from the Toronto-Dominion Bank's fund arm or its discount brokerage division, TD Waterhouse. Outside of ETFs, the e-Series offers the lowest MERs on index funds. For example, the e-Series version of the TD Canadian Index Fund has an MER of 0.31 per cent, which is an outstanding value in comparison to the 0.84 per cent charged on the regular version of this fund. It's worth noting that the comparable ETF to this index mutual fund, the iShares CDN Composite Index Fund, has an MER of 0.25 per cent. Sure, the lower MER on this ETF adds to your returns over the long term. But you have to weigh this against the fact that you can buy e-funds at no cost, while a brokerage commission will likely apply every time to add to or subtract from your ETF holdings (see Chapter Three for an important exception).

It's my sense that e-funds haven't really taken off with investors. Too bad, because they're one of the fund industry's best deals.

3. Mawer Canadian Balanced Retirement Savings

Balanced funds, as explained earlier in this chapter, are predominantly an egregiously overpriced category of fund designed for investors who prefer easy solutions over smart ones. Occasionally, though, you'll come across a balanced fund that legitimizes the idea of mixing exposure to stocks and bonds in a single fund rather than by cherry-picking separate bond and equity funds.

This fund, managed by a small but well-respected firm called Mawer Investment Management, averaged annual returns of 7.4 per cent over the twenty years leading up to the writing of this book, which is on the high side of what you might reasonably expect from a well-diversified portfolio of funds from all categories. Classified as a global equity balanced fund, Mawer Canadian Balanced Retirement Savings had about 50 per cent of its assets in stocks from around the globe—including a dominant weighting in Canada—another 37 per cent in bonds and the rest in cash.

The Mawer team of managers is first rate, but what really distinguishes this fund is its exceptionally low management expense ratio of 1 per cent. Expect an MER of double that— or more—from competing funds. One drawback: the minimum buy-in amount is $5,000. Note: This fund is designed for registered accounts. For taxable accounts, Mawer offers its Canadian Diversified Investment Fund, with a comparable MER of 1.02 per cent.

4. Beutel Goodman Canadian Equity

Consider this fund as a good example of what small, independent money managers have to offer. Truth be told, Beutel Goodman isn't really a mutual fund firm. It's best described as the blue-chip manager of $14 billion or so for wealthy individuals, pension plans, endowments and foundations. Beutel piggybacks its funds on top of these other lines of business, which ensures that investors get the same expertise as big institutional clients. It also helps keep costs low, a point that is highlighted by this fund's low management expense ratio of 1.2 per cent.

By the way, those big institutional clients like to have their money managed in a particular way. They don't go in for big bets on one sector or another, they don't want their money in small speculative stocks, and they *do* place great emphasis on protecting against crushing losses. For that reason, the portfolio of stocks this fund is likely to hold is blue-chip all the way.

No, you won't likely see this fund leading the performance charts for a given year. Consistency is the goal here, and that's what investors have received. Over the fifteen years to the writing of this book, the compound average annual return was a respectable 6.5 per cent. If you're looking for a Canadian equity fund you can buy and rely on for decades, this one's worth a look. Unfortunately, the minimum upfront investment is $10,000.

5. Trimark Fund SC

The Trimark Fund is a senior statesman among mutual funds, with a history that stretches back to 1981. The managers have changed many times over the years, and performance has been up and down, but there are three constants. One is an emphasis on buying growing, market-leading businesses that trade at reasonable prices, while another is a history of delivering above-average returns. The last is a management expense ratio that is one of the fund world's biggest bargains.

The SC in this fund's name stands for "service charge," and it refers to the fact that it's sold with an upfront sales commission.

In practice, this commission ranges from maybe one to three percentage points down to zero. The alternative is to buy the A version of the fund, which is available with a deferred sales charge and no upfront fee. The difference between the two versions is that the A option has an MER of 2.54 per cent, while SC has an MER of just 1.6 per cent. The fund-analysis firm Morningstar Canada has said in a report that SC's MER is lower than 93 per cent of its peers. This is all the more extraordinary when you consider that Invesco Trimark is a big, mainstream fund company and not one of the small firms that typically offer bargain-priced funds. A sign of sanity in the fund world: the assets in Trimark Fund SC are two and a half times those in Trimark Fund A. Amen to that.

FIVE FUNDS THAT STOOD UP TO THE BEAR

The 2001–02 stock market downturn was a nasty piece of business, but it was an all-expenses-paid trip to Disneyland in comparison to the bear market of 2008–09. In 2001–02, a goodly number of conservative mainstream mutual funds managed to deliver only minor losses or even make a bit of money. In 2008–09, the damage to fund investors was far more pervasive. In the worst phase of the decline, dozens of widely held funds were off 35 to 40 per cent on a twelve-month basis. Let's look at some of the small number of funds that managed to buck this trend.

1. IA Clarington Canadian Conservative Equity
This is one of the country's oldest mutual funds (having been around since October 1950) and also one of my favourite fund stories. At the time I was writing this book, IA Clarington

Canadian Conservative Equity was being run by a group that included George Frazer, who signed on in 1950, and Walt Tynkaluk, who came along in 1956. I've interviewed these guys a couple of times over the years because it's hard to find the long-term perspective on investing that they provide.

These guys don't just have perspective, though. They've also got chops. Their returns are consistently above average (though they sometimes lag in galloping bull markets) and they know how to protect unitholders in a down market. While the average Canadian equity fund fell 15.4 per cent in the wretched month of October 2008, theirs fell just 7 per cent. A major reason for this resilience is that the fund concentrates on strong, blue-chip dividend stocks and stays away from the kind of faddish stocks you'll see leading the market from time to time.

2. Mackenzie Ivy Canadian

A fascinating fund, and one that teaches an important lesson about how a money manager can be wrong in the short term but right in the long run. Ivy Canadian was once one of the largest Canadian mutual funds, but it bled assets in the bull market of 2003–08 because manager Jerry Javasky declined to buy energy and mining stocks in any great quantity. In performance terms, Ivy Canadian ranked in the bottom 25 per cent of its peer group for five straight years.

And then came 2008, when global recession caused commodity prices to fall and commodity stocks to do likewise. Not owning many of these stocks, Ivy Canadian sidestepped the worst of the market decline. Its loss for October 2008 was 6 per cent, a simply outstanding result achieved mainly through conservative stock selection (only 5 per cent of the fund was in cash going into the month).

Javasky retired in early 2009, but he left a team of managers that will continue to seek companies with strong competitive positions, sound management and the ability to generate above-average annual rates of growth. It's an approach that stood up extremely well during the 2001–02 bear market, too.

3. Mackenzie Ivy Foreign Equity

Jerry Javasky was the lead manager on this fund as well, and the results are even better than Ivy Canadian. This fund lost an insignificant 0.05 per cent in October 2008, which if you round it off is essentially a flat month. Meanwhile, the average peer fund in the global equity category was losing 11.3 per cent.

How shrewd was Javasky in keeping this fund in solid shape in a nasty market? Just over one per cent of the fund was exposed to the hard-hit financial sector, while 45 per cent was in a pair of classic defensive sectors, consumer staples and health care. Also, 15 per cent of the fund was in cash, a bulwark against falling markets and a resource to be deployed in snapping up quality stocks that fell in price.

For a couple of reasons, global equity funds, particularly those with heavy U.S. exposure, have been just pathetic on the whole in the past decade. A period of meteoric improvement in the Canadian dollar undercut returns generated in other currencies, and then there was the commodity boom that favoured resource-heavy markets like Canada above others. Yet for the ten-year period ending October 31, 2008, Ivy Foreign Equity had made an average annual return of 3.5 per cent—compared to an average annual *loss* of 0.4 per cent for the average global equity fund.

4. Franklin U.S. Rising Dividends

U.S. equity funds lost 30.3 per cent on average for the twelve months to December 31, 2008, a period of fiercely bearish market activity. Franklin U.S. Rising Dividends was not exempt—it fell 11.1 per cent over the same period. But its performance in October 2008, the epicentre of a storm of wealth destruction, was brilliant. The fund ended the month flat, which means its unitholders didn't lose anything amid the closest thing most market observers have seen to full-out stock market panic.

Dividend-focused funds typically have huge weightings in financial shares, which were slaughtered in 2008. But this fund kept its exposure down to just less than 20 per cent. Its biggest holdings included Walmart, a stalwart in the bear market, and Procter & Gamble, which also held up comparatively well.

This fund's mission is to invest 80 per cent of its assets in U.S. companies with a history of "consistent and substantial dividend increases," which is in theory a sound strategy because of the tendency for rising dividends to feed through to a rising share price.

5. RBC Monthly Income

This fund exemplifies a lesson about owning conservative, income-producing investments in a down market. While these securities may fall in price, and fall hard, they can still churn out regular payments of dividends, interest and such. If you're a senior in need of income, this is a comfort. And if you're a younger investor trying to build a bigger portfolio, receiving this income is like getting paid to wait for a market turnaround.

RBC Monthly Income's unit price fell 7.2 per cent in October 2008, which sounds nasty but which in fact put it among the best performers among its peers in the Canadian neutral balanced category. That's the pattern for this fund—it has lost less than most in down markets and made more in up markets.

Part of the reason for this fund's resilience is the fact that its assets are split roughly 50/50 between stocks and bonds. Expect to receive monthly income that over a year will produce a somewhat higher yield than a GIC. Given that some of the income comes from tax-advantaged dividends, you can expect a better after-tax return than GICs, as well.

FIVE FUNDS THAT WERE MAULED BY THE BEAR

Funds of all types got pounded in 2008–09, but a few stood out either because of the severity of their losses or because they were the type of fund that one might have expected to fare better. Let's look at a few hard-hit names, each of which teaches a lesson about the risks involved in owning funds.

1. TD Canadian Equity

"You play with the bull, you get the horns." I don't really like that expression, which conveys way too much know-it-all smugness. And yet, it applies perfectly to anyone left to wonder, "Wha' 'appen?" after being gored by this fund.

Heading into the stock market peak in June 2008, TD Canadian Equity was one of the most impressive performers in the country, thanks to very heavy portfolio weightings in energy, metals and fertilizers. In fact, its five-year compound average to June 30 was 22.1 per cent, great for any fund, but especially impressive for one from a big bank fund family (they tend to be a touch conservative).

The risk level in this commodity-heavy approach was apparent, but not widely heeded if you judge by the hefty $3.5 billion invested in the fund at June 30, 2008. So there must have been a lot of unhappy investors when the fund plunged in the commodity-led market devastation that followed. The damage tally in October 2008: a loss of 21.2 per cent, which was much worse than the average 15.4-per-cent decline in Canadian equity funds and, alarmingly, worse than the 16.7-per cent decline in the S&P/TSX composite index. Still, with commodities rallying in the first half of 2009, TD Canadian Equity was once again among the leaders in its peer group.

2. Mackenzie Universal Canadian Resource

The manager of this fund through 2008 was Fred Sturm, chief investment strategist at Mackenzie Financial and one of the smartest exploiters of the commodity boom of mid-decade. At one time, Sturm's unitholders made out like bandits in this fund, reaping annual returns between 2001 and 2007 that topped out at 43.8 per cent and bottomed out, if you can call it that, at 18.3 per cent.

In 2008, however, Sturm hit some kind of a wall. Mackenzie Universal Canadian Resource lost half its value in a three-month span and almost 31 per cent in October alone. Resource funds in general were annihilated in 2008, but this one was special. It's interesting to note that a few other funds managed by Sturm—Mackenzie Universal Precious Metals, Mackenzie Universal World Resource Class and Mackenzie Growth—were also hit very hard in 2008. Mackenzie Growth, a Canadian-focused equity fund, lost about 60 per cent of its value in 2008.

The fate of Mackenzie Universal Canadian Resource is a reminder that even the brightest investing minds can be smacked around in a stock market plunge. If you own a fund in a risky sector, no matter how good it is, you have to keep your exposure under strict limits.

3. AIC Advantage

In its heyday, this fund was a money-making machine fuelled by a savvy emphasis on financial stocks. Unfortunately, many of the same financial names that helped this fund soar were the ones that kneecapped it in 2008–09. Financial stocks comprised about 85 per cent of the fund as the financial crisis bit, and at one point the fund had posted a twelve-month loss of close to 50 per cent. The ten-year numbers in spring 2009 were so ugly that a decade-long investment would have turned $10,000 into less than $7,000.

The irony here is that AIC's corporate slogan was "Buy. Hold. And Prosper" (the company was bought by Manulife Financial in 2009). It's a sound approach to investing in general, but it only works when you have a well-balanced, conservatively run fund along the lines of Beutel Goodman Canadian Equity, mentioned earlier in this chapter. AIC Advantage, it's now clear, was basically a financial-services-sector fund with a modest amount of diversification into other areas. In a bull market for the financial sector, this fund could be a winner once again. But at the depths of the bear market, it was an example of how being in the wrong sector at the wrong time can cause crushing losses.

4. Dynamic Power Canadian Growth

This is a fund you'd expect to get whacked in a down market, and it more than delivered. In a three-month span in 2008, it managed to lose 44.1 per cent, exactly double what its peer funds in the Canadian-focused equity category lost on average. Should investors in this fund have been surprised by the decline? Not if they were paying attention.

Under manager Rohit Sehgal, this fund was a money-making juggernaut in the bear market that lasted from 2003 until mid-2008. From 2003 through 2007, annual returns ranged from a low of 16.7 per cent to a high of 35.6 per cent. It's the way in which Sehgal made all this money that pointed to the decline of 2008. In a word, the answer is commodities. In the summer of 2008, about 80 per cent of the fund was invested in the energy, metal and agriculture sectors, all of which were flattened as the year wore on.

Sehgal is renowned as a growth manager, which means he rides stocks that are running ahead of the pack in terms of their revenue and profit growth. In good times, expect top-flight returns from a well-run growth fund like this. In bad times, expect to get clobbered.

5. Criterion Global Clean Energy

The other funds mentioned in this section are all well-established, widely held names, whereas this fund is both small and new.

It's included here to make the point that trendy sector funds are a particular risk in a bear market.

The mutual fund industry is always looking for hot new products to bring to market and, to be honest, most are a waste of your time, not to mention your money. By the time fund industry executives spot a new trend in investing and introduce a fund to exploit it, there's a good chance the trend is well on its way to being played out. Investors who get sucked in may make a little money in the early days, but in the longer run they get beat up.

That's the story with Criterion Global Clean Energy, which was introduced in August 2007 and enjoyed some initial success before getting de-energized in the bear market. It's hard to criticize the concept on which this fund is based because clean energy will one day be a vital economic sector. In 2008, however, clean energy lost its drive as oil prices plunged and people became more worried about keeping their jobs than about their carbon footprints.

The next time oil prices surge, this fund may be in just the right spot to make some serious money for investors—if it's still around, that is.

FIVE GOOD SOCIALLY RESPONSIBLE FUNDS

Socially responsible investing means directing your money into companies that aren't in sectors like tobacco, gambling or armaments,
and that are exemplary corporate citizens in such areas as environmental policy, community involvement and corporate governance. It's
difficult for individual investors to find the most socially responsible
companies on their own, which explains the growth of socially responsible mutual funds and exchange-traded funds in the past decade.
Here are some funds that stand out for delivering solid returns as
well as a socially responsible investing experience.

1. Ethical Canadian Dividend

First and foremost, this is a very nice little Canadian dividend
fund that performs as well or better than many much larger competitors. In fact, you could easily make a case for owning this
fund based on its long-term returns. The added bonus for
socially responsible investors is that it's run by the Ethical Funds
family, which uses a corporate sustainability scorecard to evalu-
ate stocks for potential investment, emphasizing the companies'
track records on environmental, social and governance issues.

Ethical Funds, owned by the country's credit union movement, also tries to engage the companies in which they own
shares by pointing out weaknesses and suggesting solutions.

2. Ethical Special Equity

This fund is in the Canadian small- and mid-cap category, which
means it holds the shares of companies that are considered
small or medium-sized based on their market capitalization

(calculated by multiplying the number of shares outstanding by the share price). This is an inherently risky sector in which to invest, but Ethical Special Equity does a fine job of balancing risk and return.

In 2008, a year of annihilation for both small and large stocks, the fund lost 32.6 per cent, while the average loss for its peers clocked in at 40.6 per cent. Over the ten years to December 31, 2008, it made 10.6 per cent on average, while peers made 5 per cent. Again, that's a fine record for any fund, never mind one run in a socially responsible way.

3. PH&N Community Values Bond

Earlier on in this chapter, you read how one of the great bargains in fundland is the PH&N Bond Fund. PH&H Community Values Bond is run by the same group of managers, but with a focus on social responsibility. What's the point of using a socially responsible screen on a bond fund, which generally holds a lot of government-issued debt?

The answer is that this fund holds something like half of its assets in bonds issued by financially sound corporations. This should help it deliver somewhat higher returns than funds that stick to safer, but lower-yielding, government bonds.

4. Desjardins Environment

This fund, offered through Caisse Desjardins, is available only in Quebec and Ontario. At first glance, it appears to be a conventional Canadian equity product with major holdings that, at the time of writing, included EnCana, Royal Bank, Potash Corporation of Saskatchewan and Rogers Communications.

However, Desjardins says stocks for the fund are selected with an eye toward environmentally conscious companies. Returns have been comfortably above the average over the long term for Canadian equity funds, but the fund did struggle in the second half of 2008.

5. iShares CDN Jantzi Social Index Fund

This exchange-traded fund (see Chapter Three for much more on ETFs) is based on the Jantzi Social Index, which is made up of sixty big corporations that have scored well according to environmental, social and governance rating criteria. Jantzi Research is a company that specializes in screening companies to find the most socially responsible names.

Jantzi Research has a hand in the running of several socially responsible investment funds in this country. One of them is the Meritas Jantzi Social Index Fund, which does pretty much the same thing as the iShares Jantzi ETF. The difference is that the Meritas fund should be available wherever mutual funds are sold, whereas the iShares ETF must be purchased through a brokerage (the stock symbol is XEN). Also, the Meritas fund has a management expense ratio of 1.94 per cent, while the iShares ETF is a much lower 0.5 per cent.

**FIVE REASONS TO DO WHAT NO INVESTOR HAS DONE BEFORE:
READ A MUTUAL FUND PROSPECTUS AND A MANAGEMENT
REPORT ON FUND PERFORMANCE**

Mutual fund companies are required by regulatory authorities to produce exhaustively detailed descriptions of their products. Among these documents are the simplified prospectuses and the semi-annual management report on fund performance, both of which make for utterly fascinating reading. No, I am not suffering from personal finance columnist fatigue, and neither am I trying to suck up to the fund industry (as if!). Honestly, I think fund prospectuses and management reports are worth reading because of all the information they offer—information, I should add, that is essential in helping you choose the right funds for your needs.

1. You can see how fees have changed over the years.

Canada's fund industry has been criticized for having among the highest fees in the world. But for the most part, fees have definitely fallen over the past several years. Want to make sure the funds you own are part of the trend? Check the Financial Highlights area of your fund's management report on fund performance. There, you'll find MER data for the most recent period, as well as the five previous years.

2. You can find out how much trading the fund manager does, and how much it's costing you.

Near the MER data in the Financial Highlights area of the management report on fund performance is something called "portfolio turnover rate." This is an expression of how much trading the manager does. A 100-per-cent portfolio turnover rate means the trading activity in the fund is equivalent to replacing all the stocks in the portfolio over the course of a year. What does the portfolio turnover rate mean to you in practical terms? Check the trading expense ratio (TER) number nearby. As described earlier in this chapter, it tells you how much of your returns are being eaten up by trading costs.

3. You can find out how much your adviser or investment dealer gets paid for selling a fund.

Head to the Dealer Compensation section of a fund prospectus and you'll get the lowdown on the sales fees an adviser or dealer is allowed to charge for a particular fund, and on the trailing commissions they receive as compensation for ongoing client service. This is essential data in deciding what kind of value you're getting from a fund investment.

4. You can find out about miscellaneous other fees.

Some mutual fund families give advisers and dealers the latitude to charge fees for moving a client's money from one fund to another in the same family (this is called switching). There can also be fees associated with short-term trading, which means selling in the first couple of months after you make your investment.

5. You can find out what's in your fund.

The profiles of each fund on Globeinvestor.com include lists of their top ten holdings; in some cases, these are updated monthly. For a look at a fund's top twenty-five holdings, consult the quarterly portfolio also updates that fund companies issue. Have you read about problems in one particular sector of the economy, or the stock market? This is the place to go to see if your fund is exposed.

THREE

NAVIGATING THE STOCK MARKET

THE STOCK MARKET IS WHERE YOU GO in order to make higher returns than you can get from virtually risk-free bonds and guaranteed investment certificates. On average, you can expect to make 6 to 8 per cent annually in stocks, and there will be years when you hit double digits. Of course, there will be years when you lose in double digits, too (like I have to tell you that after the lovely year of 2008). Be humble when you invest in stocks, keep risk in mind at all times and understand that navigating the market is a learning process that never ends.

THREE OVERSIMPLIFICATIONS ABOUT STOCK MARKET INVESTING THAT YOU'LL RUN INTO CONSTANTLY

There's a common body of wisdom in the investing world that, for the most part, is built on decades of experience and observation. The problem for people absorbing this wisdom is that it's often massaged to benefit those who sell investment advice or products. That's not to say that this wisdom is wrong. Oversimplified is probably a better way of putting it.

1. "Buy and hold" is the best approach for the average investor.

On the surface, buying and holding is an investing strategy that will serve you well. The problem is that some people take "buy and hold" as a call to remain passive when action is required to fix a troubled portfolio.

But let's be clear: left to their own devices, investors fiddle around with their portfolios way too much. They make the elementary error of buying funds coming off great years, and they sell after a year or two, as the fund falls back to earth. The net result is that they have bought high and sold low.

Buying and holding is based on the idea that stocks and funds go up and down over a long period of time—let's say ten years, at least—but the highs will outweigh the lows and provide you with returns that, for stocks, should average about 6 to 8 per cent.

The bear market that took hold in the latter part of 2008 challenged the buy-and-hold theory of investing. Investors were told not to panic and sell, but in retrospect selling would have been the right move. People who sold stocks at the beginning of October 2008 could have protected themselves against the ghastly double-digit losses of the next few months.

So, what's the best approach—buying and holding or trying to time market ups and downs?

The correct answer is something I'll call "intelligent buy-and-hold investing." Others call it rebalancing. You start by determining the correct mix of investments for your needs and risk tolerance, and you maintain it through market ups and downs by judiciously buying and selling to keep things in balance. When the markets are soaring, you have to keep your exposure to stocks under strict control by selling some of your holdings. If your stocks or equity funds were 50 per cent of your portfolio and now they're 60 per cent, sell to get back to 50 per cent. If your stocks or equity funds fall to 40 per cent, it's time to buy.

The idea here is, first, to avoid the buy-and-hold passivity that leads investors to walk face-first into the bear market buzzsaw and, second, to avoid amateur-hour guessing about what the market is going to do. Have a plan, and follow it.

2. Asset allocation is what really matters in building a portfolio.

It's not unusual to hear investment industry types go on and on about how asset allocation—the mix of stocks, bonds and cash in a portfolio—is the main driver of portfolio returns. In fact, academic studies have shown that asset allocation is vitally important to determining portfolio returns, particularly for long-term investing. But choosing good stocks, mutual funds and exchange-traded funds is important, too.

One reason why the investment industry pushes the concept of asset allocation is to wise up investors so they understand that they need a mix of things in their portfolios, not just a grab bag of whatever types of assets seem to be working at the moment. This is useful. But I have a sneaking feeling that the emphasis on asset allocation is also a way of blowing smoke over the rotten performance of so many mutual funds. By going on and on about how the mix of investments is of primary importance, clients may pay less attention to individual funds that are devouring fees but producing little.

The truth of asset allocation is that it's a surprisingly nebulous concept. Try comparing the mixes recommended for your personal finance situation by various investing websites or software packages (investment advisers use these). I tried this and received vastly different blueprints. Some recommended foreign bonds, others didn't. Some recommended having a lot of U.S. exposure, others didn't. Some stressed having significant exposure to small-cap stocks, others didn't. The point is that there's no black-and-white correct answer to the question of how you should design a portfolio. So work in broad strokes. Consider your age, risk, tolerance, investing goals and time until retirement. Then, research a few different options and choose one that you think you can live with.

Note that asset allocation is a matter an investment adviser should spend a fair amount of time on. If you're a self-directed investor, most online brokers now offer portfolio-planning tools that develop asset mixes based on client needs.

3. The smart way to invest is in partnership with an adviser.

It's quite possible that you would be best served by having an investment adviser. Maybe you don't know much about investing at all. Or maybe you know a fair bit but don't have the time or the interest to look after your portfolio. Advisers, at their best, are great simplifiers. Think along the lines of having an accountant at tax time. Just as you take all your tax receipts to the accountant and expect a tidy tax return, so you can take all your investment issues to an adviser and expect a tidy investment portfolio to be created.

So why invest for yourself when experts who can do it for you are ubiquitous? The main reason is the opportunity to design a portfolio that is at least as efficient and, quite probably, cheaper than an adviser. The background here is that advisers must be paid for the work they do, and rightly so. This payment is sometimes made directly by clients to advisers, but more often it's embedded in the cost of buying and owning investment products. Those costs cut into your returns and, if you eliminate them, you stand to make higher returns.

Let's remember that advisers can stop you from making any number of boneheaded moves that will undermine your returns. Then again, advisers aren't immune to these errors themselves. It's entirely possible that an adviser will collect fees from you that reduce returns that have been further undermined by bad decision-making. The point here is that having an adviser is not a free pass to tip-top investment returns. If you can invest for yourself effectively, and you not only want to but have the time, give it some thought.

BEYOND MUTUAL FUNDS: THREE ESSENTIAL PORTFOLIO BUILDING BLOCKS

Many investors and advisers use mutual funds to build portfolios, and that's fine. There are lots of reasons to criticize mutual funds (see Chapter Two), but at their best they're a very good way for the average person to invest over a lifetime. Why look beyond funds? Because there are simple alternatives out there that are cheaper and thus offer the potential for superior returns.

1. Blue-Chip Dividend Stocks

What the stock market giveth, it can take away. You'll know this if you ever bought a stock, watched it climb and then saw it plunge below your purchase price. Dividends, on the other hand, are for keeps. Sure, a company can suspend or reduce its dividend if it runs into problems (U.S. companies seem to do this more than Canadian ones), but this is rare. Recessions aside, most dividend-paying companies can be counted on to put cash in the hands of shareholders every quarter, regardless of what is happening to the share price.

The New York Times ran an article during a particularly nasty period for the markets in 2008 saying that dividends have historically accounted for 40 per cent of the U.S. stock market's total returns (share price appreciation plus dividends). The article went on to say that since the 1990s, thanks to a pair of bear markets, dividends were the source of the only gains to be had from stocks.

You'll fall in love with your dividend stocks when you start noticing how they keep shovelling cash into your portfolio at times when they and most every other stock are plunging in price. You'll love them even more when you notice how your premium dividend stocks keep increasing the amount of cash they pay out over time. In my own portfolio, I have stocks whose dividends have risen to the point that the yields on the upfront cost of the shares are in double digits. Just so you know, a stock's dividend yield is calculated by dividing the annual dividend by the stock price and then multiplying by 100.

There are two other benefits to dividends. One is that they're taxed much more favourably than interest income in a non-registered account thanks to the dividend tax credit. Another is a little-discussed phenomenon whereby a company's shares tend to rise over time by a similar magnitude as its dividends increase. There isn't an exact correlation, and in some cases there's no correlation at all. But there is a clear pattern among many stocks indicating that an average 10 per cent annual increase in the dividend will feed through to a similar rise in the share price. Rising dividends are a bullish sign about a company—that's probably the best explanation.

2. Exchange-Traded Funds (ETFs)

ETFs were an "it" investing product in the mid- to late 2000s and, to be honest, the investing industry went a little crazy with them. According to the money management firm Hahn Investment Stewards, the number of ETFs listed on stock exchanges around the world went from 21 in 1997 to 1,171 at the end of 2007. The result: an intimidating and confusing level of choice was brought to a type of investment that was once the picture of simplicity and practicality.

ETFs started out as a way for investors to tap into the returns of major stock indexes using a nice, convenient package that traded like a stock. Owning ETFs, then, is like owning a miniature version of the index. Your returns equal whatever the index gains or loses, minus a fee that looks like a bargain compared to conventional mutual funds. Those low fees are a key reason for buying ETFs. Fact is, many mutual funds deliver returns that are well below the stock indexes they use to gauge their performance. Sometimes this is a result of sloppy management, (technically known as "tracking error") and sometimes it's those high fees. By buying directly into the index, you're assured of making what the index does, minus a bit for fees.

As I was writing this book, the average Canadian equity fund's compound average annual three- and ten-year returns were minus-10.6 per cent and 3.7 per cent, respectively. This compared with minus-8.9 per cent for the S&P/TSX composite total return index, including dividends, over the three-year period, and 4.6 per cent for the ten-year period (rotten numbers, for sure, but the bear market was in full force).

ETFs, remember, give you index returns minus fees, for the most part, of 0.17 to 0.65 per cent. So let's take the three-year returns for the S&P/TSX composite and reduce them by 0.40 per cent, the average of the two extremes. We're left with minus-9.3 per cent for the three-year period and 4.2 per cent for the ten years, both still ahead of the average fund.

One other ETF attribute you'll like: despite the product clutter (keep reading this chapter for help in sorting through it), you can easily build and maintain a sensible portfolio with a minimum of effort. It's really a matter of selecting a few ETF portfolio building blocks and assembling them in a way that suits your needs.

QuickSurvey: Let's Review the Benefits of ETFs

Low Fees: They're a fraction of what mutual funds charge, which means less of a drag on returns.

Variety: There are hundreds of ETFs available to North American investors and, while many are too esoteric to bother with, there are lots of choices for building sound and simple portfolios.

Intra-Day Liquidity: A fancy term that means you can buy ETFs at any time when the stock markets are open, whereas mutual funds are sold at the end-of-day unit price if you buy in before 2:30 p.m. or thereabouts, and at the next day's closing price if you buy after that time.

Transparency: Holdings are posted on the Internet and updated on a daily basis, whereas mutual funds must show clients what they hold only periodically.

Diversification: Like a sector? Buy the corresponding ETF and you're done.

Tax Efficiency: ETFs replicate stock indexes, which usually make only minor changes each year and thus generate only minor trading requirements for those running ETFs; mutual funds often do more trading, which potentially means higher taxable capital-gains distributions (in taxable accounts) at the end of the year.

Accessibility: Any ETF listed on a North American exchange is readily available, and you can buy as little as one share if you want to.

3. Individual Bonds and Guaranteed Investment Certificates (GICs)

Bonds and GICs are covered in greater depth in Chapter Four, but let's look at them briefly here. If you're investing for a goal—say, retirement or your children's education—you'll want fixed-income investments like these in your portfolio. Not because they'll help you make more money over the long term, but because they'll make you a happier, more complete investor. Bonds and GICs don't return all that much in this era of low interest rates, but they offer stability at times when the stock markets are plunging. You can talk all you want about how risk-tolerant you are, but you'll be a lot more comfortable in a bear market if you own bonds and GICs. You'll also be a lot more likely to stick to your investing plan and not make a precipitous and foolish decision to sell good stocks and funds that are down in price.

DIVIDEND BULLDOGS: A DOZEN COMPANIES THAT RAISED THEIR DIVIDENDS IN TOUGH TIMES

Dividends are an underappreciated investing marvel—free money paid into your account every quarter by companies, regardless of whether their share prices go up, down or sideways. But don't make the mistake of classifying all dividend stocks as more or less the same. There are actually two classes, the first being companies that pay a dividend that rarely, or never, increases. The second encompasses companies that are so well run and consistent in their performance that they can ramp up their dividends as frequently as every couple of quarters in good economic times. What's more impressive than a company that raises its dividend regularly? How about a company that raised its cash payout amid some of the worst economic conditions in recent memory? Here are some companies that did just that in 2008 and 2009. Note: Stock symbols include the exchange on which they trade (TSX=Toronto Stock Exchange; NYSE=New York Stock Exchange).

1. BCE (BCE-TSX)

Back in 2008, this telecom giant was supposed to have been taken private in a deal that would have paid shareholders a handsome $42.75 per share. In early 2009, with investors still smarting from the deal's collapse, BCE management pushed through a small but significant 5-per-cent increase in the dividend. The message: BCE is trying to make it up to shareholders who were disappointed when the deal fell apart and the company's shares fell back to the $25 range. BCE has never been one of the country's more dynamic dividend growth stocks, but it does offer a high degree of dividend safety thanks to its status as a telephone utility.

2. Canadian National Railway (CNR-TSX)

This former Crown corporation was created in 1919 and is now one of the largest railroads in North America. CN is also widely regarded as one of the better dividend growth stocks in the Canadian market, a reputation that was enhanced when it bumped up its payout by 10 per cent in early 2009. As the company noted at the time, this marked the thirteenth straight time since the company went public in 1995 that it had delivered a double-digit percentage increase in its dividend.

3. Enbridge (ENB–TSX)

This pipeline and energy-distribution company has been paying dividends for more than fifty-five years and has increased its cash payouts by an average 10 per cent annually over that period. There was a nine-year period from the mid-1980s to the mid-1990s where the dividend remained static, but there have been annual hikes since then that have more than doubled the amount of money paid out per quarter.

4. Fortis (FTS–TSX)

When Canada's largest publicly traded distributor of electricity and natural gas raised its dividend amid the depressed market conditions of early 2009, it marked the thirty-sixth straight year in which the company's cash payout had increased. Oh, and with pretty much the entire universe unravelling in 2008, Fortis managed its best-ever annual profit. Like Enbridge, Fortis is a defensive stock that you're glad to own when the overall stock market is plunging.

5. Rogers Communications (RCI.B–TSX)

This telecom giant has recently been developing a profile as a dividend growth stock. Amid tough economic conditions, and challenging times for the company itself, Rogers bumped up its quarterly dividend by 16 per cent in early 2009. Impressively, that increase still left the company with plenty of cash to invest in its operations.

6. Shaw Communications (SJR.B–TSX)

This western Canadian cable television company has one of the more outstanding dividend growth records in the country. From August 2008 through March 2009, Shaw bumped up its monthly dividend not once, but twice. Shaw is a rarity in paying cash to shareholders on a monthly basis.

7. SNC-Lavalin Group (SNC-TSX)

You may not have heard of this Montreal-based engineering and construction firm, but it's a global success story with operations in a hundred countries or so. The dividend history can be summed as two decades of regular increases, including one announced in the first quarter of 2009, a period when you'd expect companies involved in construction to be struggling against poor economic conditions.

8. Toronto-Dominion Bank (TD-TSX)

The global financial crisis hit hard in 2008 and, while Canadian banks were considered among the world's healthiest, they still suffered through a period of writedowns and troubled loans. Nevertheless, TD stood tall. The bank actually raised its dividend twice in 2008, bringing it to 61 cents per quarter from 57 cents. Not a big total increase overall, but an impressive sign of stability and confidence from TD in its underlying businesses.

9. TransCanada Corp. (TRP-TSX)

Back in 1999, TransCanada shocked and angered investors by cutting its dividend. The company has annually increased its dividend since then, and it didn't miss a beat in the rotten economic conditions of 2009. That's the kind of dividend reliability you'd expect from a company involved in stable operations like running pipelines and power-generating plants.

10. Walmart (WMT-NYSE)

The focus so far has been on Canadian dividend stocks, but it's worth throwing Walmart into the mix because it was a big-time clutch performer in the economic downturn that delivered a dividend increase at a time when other retailers were in survival mode.

11. 3M Co. (MMM)

The maker of Scotch tape, Post-it Notes and all kinds of industrial and high-tech products has increased its dividends for fifty-one consecutive years. The increase in early 2009 was by a token amount—just one cent—but for those who aren't impressed, it's worth noting that General Electric, another industrial behemoth with a strong dividend history, had to slash its quarterly payout in early 2009.

12. Diebold (DBD–NYSE)

This maker of ATMs used by the banking industry announced its fifty-sixth straight annual dividend increase in early 2009. The total increase was just 4 per cent, but give this company full marks for the kind of consistency seen all too infrequently in the corporate world.

FIVE MORE DIVIDEND GROWTH STOCKS YOU SHOULD KNOW ABOUT

The following companies have sterling long-term dividend-growth records. The names on the list that are in the financial sector struggled in the global financial crisis of 2008–09, and there were lingering questions as of press time about whether some might have to cut their dividend.

1. Royal Bank of Canada (RY-TSX)

Because of problems related to exposure to U.S. real estate and an economic slowdown across North America, RBC had gone a full six quarters as of press time without a dividend increase. That's unusual, because this bank's usual pattern has been to bump up the quarterly payout every couple of quarters or so. The investment dealer UBS Securities Canada found that RBC's compound average annual dividend growth rate from 2004 through 2009 was 14.6 per cent, tops among the Big Six Canadian banks.

2. Bank of Nova Scotia (BNS-TSX)

Scotiabank calls itself Canada's most international bank, based on the fact that it has operations in places like Mexico, the Caribbean and South and Central America. Combine this with its extensive Canadian operations and you have a business that runs well enough to have produced average dividend growth of 12.2 per cent annually between 2004 and 2009, according to UBS. It's worth noting that while most of the big banks had to temporarily throttle back on dividend increases in 2008, Scotiabank and the Toronto-Dominion Bank were able to bump up their quarterly cash payouts slightly.

3. Power Financial (PWF–TSX)

Power Financial is a holding company with interests in the likes of mutual fund giant IGM Financial, Great-West Lifeco (Canada's second-largest insurer), London Life Insurance Company, Canada Life Assurance Company and Putnam Investments, a U.S. fund company. All of these names were hurt in the bear market, but Power has a long history of outstanding dividend growth behind it.

4. Reitmans (RET.A–TSX)

In a sense, this is a riskier pick than some because retailing is such a cyclical business. And yet, Reitmans is a well-run, savvy outfit that, having been founded in 1926, has been around long enough to have weathered a few recessions. The company has paid a dividend for close to fifty years and is conservatively run from a financial point of view.

5. Johnson & Johnson (JNJ–NYSE)

As this book was being written, Johnson & Johnson's dividend history showed an unbroken string of annual dividend increases dating back to 1972. This stock has also outperformed the S&P 500 index over the long term.

FIVE ESSENTIAL EXCHANGE-TRADED FUNDS

As you read earlier, ETFs are cheap to own, versatile and so plentiful that you can easily get bogged down in the details when trying to select the right ones for your needs. Here are five basic ETF building blocks you can use to assemble a well-diversified, low-maintenance portfolio. Stock symbols—remember, ETFs are index trackers that trade like stocks—are provided, along with the corresponding stock exchanges (TSX=Toronto Stock Exchange; NYSE=New York Stock Exchange).

1. iShares CDN LargeCap 60 Index Fund (XIU–TSX)

Far and away the most popular ETF in the Canadian market, XIU is a way of investing in an index of large Canadian blue-chip companies called the S&P/TSX 60. All the big banks and insurance companies are members, as are big oil companies, the tech giant Research in Motion, resource stocks ranging from EnCana to Potash Corporation of Saskatchewan, and other household names like Shoppers Drug Mart and Rogers Communications. You could certainly buy the shares of these companies individually. Or you could have them wrapped together into one neat package, the XIU.

The cost of owning this fund is as low as you'll get in the Canadian ETF market, thanks to a management expense ratio of 0.17 per cent. By comparison, the largest Canadian equity mutual funds have MERs in the range of 2 per cent. Of course, you'll need to pay a brokerage commission to buy this and all other ETFs—figure on $5 to $29 for a discount broker, depending on which firm you use and how large your account is.

The XIU is the flagship product for iShares, which dominates the ETF sector in Canada and is a major player globally as well. iShares is a huge multinational operation, and you can buy its ETFs with complete confidence. Why do I say that? Two reasons, the first being that all assets in an ETF, like a mutual fund, are held separately from those of the company that offers them. If the company falls into trouble, the ETF assets should remain safe. The second reason is that, for the most part, a share of an ETF represents fractional ownership stakes in the shares of companies in an index. So there's actual value backing an ETF.

Alternative Choices: The iShares CDN Composite Index Fund (XIC–TSX), which tracks the broader S&P/TSX composite index; the Claymore Canadian Fundamental Index ETF (CRQ–TSX), which uses a unique indexing strategy that puts somewhat more emphasis on undervalued Canadian stocks.

2. iShares CDN Bond Index Fund (XBB–TSX)

This ETF is a good alternative to conventional bond mutual funds, and it may be a better bet than holding a portfolio of individual bonds, too. First off, XBB tracks an index that is designed to mirror the entire Canadian bond market, including federal and provincial bonds, corporate bonds and municipal bonds. This means you'll get a little more yield than straight government bonds, but also a high level of assurance that your quarterly interest payments will arrive without any hitches.

Another benefit is that iShares will quite likely be able to buy bonds at lower prices than you. Lower prices paid for bonds

mean higher yields—the two variables move in opposite directions. Ownership costs are yet another benefit. The MER for
this fund is 0.30 per cent, compared to 1 to almost 2 per cent
for the most popular bond mutual funds.

You can call this ETF a substitute for owning a diversified
portfolio of top-quality bonds, but there is one crucial difference between it and individual bonds. Whereas a bond will
eventually mature and return your capital to you, a bond ETF
just keeps going and going. You have to sell it like a stock when
you want to get out, and the price will depend in large part
on the interest-rate situation of the moment. Rising rates will
depress the prices of a bond ETF (and both bond mutual funds
and individual bonds), while falling rates will move the price
higher. In any case, you still get the same interest payments
that real bonds pay.

Alternative Choices: The iShares family has a variety of more specialized bond ETFs that cover areas like short- and long-term bonds,
government and corporate bonds.

3. Claymore 1–5 Year Laddered Government Bond ETF (CLF–TSX)

Whereas the iShares CDN Bond Index Fund gives you the
entire bond market in a single purchase, this fund focuses on
short- and medium-term government bonds. That's the safest
place in the bond market, which means this ETF is for risk-
averse investors who put a high premium on safety and are
willing to give up a bit of yield to get it.

You've heard of bond laddering, right? That's where you
divide your holdings in bonds or guaranteed investment certificates into equal amounts that are invested in maturities of

one through five years. The net result: you always have a certain amount of money coming due each year, which means there's cash to invest if rates are rising, and you're protected against having to renew all your money if rates fall.

This ETF tracks the DEX 1–5 Year Government Bond Index, which is made up of bonds issued by federal and provincial governments and agencies. Claymore said the index has been constructed to exactly reflect the process by which an investment adviser would maintain a bond ladder for a client, which means it is rebalanced annually.

There's an obvious benefit to this ETF in terms of simplifying the process of laddering. A more subtle benefit comes in the yield, which should be higher than most investors would get from setting up a ladder of bonds on their own. The reasoning here is that Claymore, as a large institutional investor, will pay less to buy bonds for its fund and thus enjoy higher yields. Prices, of course, move inversely to yield. Pay less, get more—that's all you need to know.

Alternative Choices: The iShares CDN Short Bond Index Fund (XSB–TSX) is a somewhat similar product, but the MER of 0.25 per cent makes it pricier than the Claymore Laddered Bond ETF, at 0.15 per cent.

4. iShares CDN MSCI EAFE 100% Hedged to CAD Dollars Index Fund (XIN–TSX)

The EAFE index from Morgan Stanley Capital International is best thought of as an "everywhere but North America" stock index (EAFE stands for Europe, Australasia and Far East). Buy this single ETF, then, and you're getting the international stock market exposure that all investors are supposed to have.

An important thing to be aware of with this ETF is that it provides currency hedging, which means it uses financial tools called derivatives to eliminate the distortions that currency movements have on investments in foreign countries. Whatever the EAFE index makes, that's what *you* make, with a little taken off to cover fees. Hedging is a good thing in times like 2007 and early 2009, when the Canadian dollar is soaring and thereby reducing returns made in foreign currencies. If the loonie is on the decline, however, hedging will reduce your returns somewhat.

If you plan on investing for ten or twenty years, hedging isn't really necessary. Research shows that over periods this long, currency ups and downs cancel each other out. For shorter time frames, hedging is a good way to ensure you make what foreign stock indexes make, with nothing lost or added because of currency moves.

If you prefer not to hedge, try a version of this ETF that is listed on the New York Stock Exchange, the iShares MSCI EAFE Index Fund (EFA–NYSE). Canadian investors can buy NYSE-listed ETFs and stocks through any broker. A bonus with this ETF: it's a little cheaper to own than the comparable Canadian iShares fund thanks to an MER that comes in at 0.35 per cent instead of 0.49 per cent.

Alternative Choices: The Claymore family of ETFs includes a fund called the International Fundamental Index ETF (CIE-TSX) that uses a slightly different indexing approach than the iShares EAFE funds. To make a long story short, the Claymore product emphasizes undervalued stocks more than the iShares one. The Claymore international ETF was too new as this book was being written to draw any conclusions about how this pattern has actually played out.

5. Vanguard Total Stock Market ETF (VTI–NYSE)

There are lots of different ETFs you can use to cover off the all-important U.S. stock market, and if you asked five experts, you'd likely get five different answers. My suggestion is an ETF from the Vanguard family, which is famous for having pioneered low-cost index investing in the United States.

There are two great things about this ETF, the first being its staggeringly low cost of ownership. The management expense ratio is 0.09 per cent, which as far as I can tell is the lowest around for retail investors in the ETF universe. It's worth noting that the average U.S. equity mutual fund has an MER of about 2.6 per cent. What would you rather own: a fund that gives up 2.6 percentage points in returns to pay fees, or one that give up just 0.09 of a point?

The second benefit of the Vanguard total market ETF is its scope. It covers off the same large stocks as the widely followed S&P 500 index, plus mid-size and small stocks. The underlying stock index is the MSCI U.S. Broad Market Index, which represents 95 per cent of the market value of companies listed on the major U.S. stock exchanges. The benefit of this broad approach is that you get some exposure to smaller-cap stocks, which tend to provide higher returns (and more risk) than big blue-chips, but you also get the stability of those blue-chips.

There is no hedging with this ETF, so your returns would be affected by moves in the Canada–U.S. exchange rate. In this case, a falling Canadian dollar is good, a rising currency is bad.

Alternative Choices: There's a hedged S&P 500 ETF listed on the Toronto Stock Exchange called the iShares CDN S&P 500 Hedged to Canadian Dollars Index Fund (XSP–TSX), and an unhedged version listed on the New York Stock Exchange called the iShares S&P 500 Index Fund (IVV–NYSE). Claymore has a hedged U.S.-market ETF listed on the Toronto market, and it's called the U.S. Fundamental Index C$ Hedged ETF (CLU–TSX).

THREE WAYS TO USE THESE SAME FIVE ETFs
TO BUILD A PORTFOLIO

Your personal mix of investments depends on factors like your age, risk tolerance and personal financial goals, so consider the asset allocation models that follow merely as illustrations of how ETFs might conceivably be combined to create a portfolio. Adjustments will be needed to suit your own needs. Stock symbols are provided (TSX=Toronto Stock Exchange; NYSE=New York Stock Exchange).

1. The Conservative Growth Portfolio

Mix: 50 per cent stocks, 50 per cent bonds

Concept: Half the portfolio benefits from the long-term growth potential of the stock market, while the other half is anchored by the stability and income offered by bonds.

Assemble it yourself with:

ETF	Ticker Symbol	MER (%)	Portfolio Weightlifting
iShares CDN LargeCap 60 Index Fund	XIU–TSX	0.17	30%
iShares CDN MSCI EAFE 100%			
Hedged to CAD Dollars Index Fund	XIN–TSX	0.49	10%
Vanguard Total Stock Market ETF	VTI–NYSE	0.09	10%
iShares CDN Bond Index Fund	XBB–TSX	0.30	50%

2. The Aggressive Growth Portfolio

Mix: 80 per cent stocks, 20 per cent bonds

Concept: Heavy on stocks, but with a reasonable level of bond exposure for stability in lean times for the stock markets.

Assemble it yourself with:

ETF	Ticker Symbol	MER (%)	Portfolio Weighting
iShares CDN LargeCap 60 Index Fund	XIU–TSX	0.17	50%
iShares CDN MSCI EAFE 100%			
Hedged to CAD Dollars Index Fund	XIN–TSX	0.49	15%
Vanguard Total Stock Market ETF	VTI–NYSE	0.09	15%
iShares CDN Bond Index Fund	XBB–TSX	0.30	20%

3. The "Better Safe than Sorry" Portfolio

Mix: 80 per cent bonds, 20 per cent stocks

Concept: Bonds account for most of this portfolio, so you'll preserve your investment capital.

Assemble it yourself with:

ETF	Ticker Symbol	MER (%)	Portfolio Weighting
The Claymore 1–5 Year Laddered	CLF–TSX	0.15	30%
Government Bond ETF			
iShares CDN Bond Index Fund	XBB–TSX	0.30	50%
iShares CDN LargeCap 60 Index Fund	XIU–TSX	0.17	15%
Vanguard Total Stock Market ETF	VTI–NYSE	0.09	5%

FIVE MORE HANDY ETFs FOR YOUR CONSIDERATION

Here are some more ETFs that can be worked into the portfolios of mainstream investors. These funds provide exposure to some niches that may or may not be covered by the preceding list of ETFs.

1. Claymore 1–5 Year Laddered Corporate Bond ETF (CBO–TSX)
Corporate bonds generally offer higher yields than government bonds because they present a higher risk profile. In 2008–09, the gap between these two types of bonds got much wider than usual, a situation that generated a lot of buzz among investing pros. The reason: an opportunity to lock in yields that were far higher than government bonds, and to realize some capital gains when the corporate bond market eventually bounced back.

Claymore Investments introduced this product in early 2009 as a competitor to the iShares CDN Corporate Bond Index Fund (XCB). Think of it as a higher-risk, higher-return complement to the aforementioned Claymore 1–5 Year Laddered Government Bond ETF. The goal here is to provide a laddered corporate-bond portfolio with a single low-cost purchase. The management expense ratio was set at a reasonable 0.25 per cent, which at the time compared to 0.40 for the iShares product.

Another difference between these two ETFs is that the Claymore product held short-term bonds. Short-term bonds are generally less risky than long-term bonds, and this is all the more true in the corporate sector. The longer a company's bonds have to go until maturity, the more uncertainty there is about whether it will remain financially strong enough to keep paying interest on schedule.

2. Claymore S&P/TSX CDN Preferred Share ETF (CPD–TSX)

You can get the full lowdown on preferred shares later in this chapter, but here's a quick rundown. Preferred shares are primarily dividend-paying vehicles, and they don't fluctuate as much in price as the common shares that are what people think of when they talk about the stock market.

In terms of risk, preferred shares fall somewhere between bonds and common shares. If a company had to conserve cash, it might typically cut or suspend the common-share dividend before touching the preferred dividend. The preferred dividend would go bye-bye before interest payments to bondholders were affected.

If any of this piques your interest in preferred shares to generate income, then take a look at the Claymore S&P/TSX Canadian Preferred Share ETF. It holds a diversified portfolio of preferred shares, which saves you the trouble of trying to make sense of individual preferred share issues. And, believe me, this can be troublesome due to the complexities involved with preferred shares. Expect yields in the 4 to 5 per cent range, which in non-registered accounts looks especially good because of the dividend tax credit. One proviso with this ETF is that it has been heavily dominated by financial stocks.

3) iShares CDN Russell 2000 Index—Canadian Dollar Hedged Index Fund (XSU–TSX)

The Russell 2000 Index is a widely followed gauge for small companies listed on U.S. exchanges. This is a component of the market that you don't get exposure to through ETFs that invest in the S&P 500, which is strictly made up of large companies. Why would you want to invest in smaller companies, which are riskier?

The answer is that some investing theorists have found that you get superior performance over the long term from small stocks as opposed to big ones. Mind the risks, though; in the bear market days of 2008 and 2009, the Russell 2000 Index did somewhat worse than the S&P 500 or the Dow Jones Industrial Average.

This ETF from the iShares family has a reasonable MER of 0.35 per cent and provides currency hedging, so that fluctuations in the Canadian dollar don't distort the returns made by the underlying index. Use this ETF as a complement to an S&P 500 ETF.

4. iShares CDN Energy Sector Index Fund (XEG–TSX)

Let's face it: Canada's economy is resource-based, and that's a good thing if you buy into the arguments about how demand for oil and metals is going to rise over the long term at rates that exceed new supplies coming online.

This ETF is a simple, convenient way to buy exposure to Canada's energy-producing giants. Almost half of this ETF's underlying index is made up of EnCana, Suncor Energy and Canadian Natural Resources. There are many smaller energy companies as well.

The MER for this ETF is somewhat pricey at 0.55 per cent, but that's much better than what you'd pay to own a natural resources or energy mutual fund.

5. iShares CDN MSCI Emerging Markets Index Fund (EEM–NYSE)

Emerging markets offer higher returns than developed

markets, but there are also far greater risks associated with them. Put another way, you stand to make outsized returns in good markets from an ETF like this, but take especially grievous losses in a bear market.

If you're still interested, this ETF is worth a look, even though the MER is flat-out expensive at 0.72 per cent. More than twenty countries are represented in the index tracked by this ETF, but China, Brazil, Korea and Taiwan dominate.

Some experts believe that Brazil, China, India and Russia are the key developing economies, and that explains why there's an emerging market sub-category focusing on these four countries. If you like that approach, then consider the Claymore BRIC ETF, which trades on the Toronto Stock Exchange under the symbol CBQ. This fund charges fees of 0.6 per cent, and it uses currency hedging for its exposure to U.S. dollars. That's key because this fund holds American Depositary Receipts (ADRs) issued by companies from the BRIC countries. ADRs are certificates that represent shares of foreign companies, priced in U.S. dollars and traded on U.S. exchanges.

Note: iShares has introduced a TSX-listed version of this ETF. The stock symbol is XEM.

THREE INTERESTING SECTORS TO CONSIDER
FOR YOUR PORTFOLIO

Playing around with sector investing combines the potential for outsized returns with the risk of losses that can shock you. So be careful about jumping into narrow investing niches. Limit your exposure to 5 per cent of your portfolio at most (less is fine) and consider sectors that pension fund managers and other pros favour. Here are a few such sectors.

1. Infrastructure

Infrastructure investing got a lot of attention in 2009 when governments moved to support their sagging economies by throwing money into building highways, bridges and other projects. But pension funds have long been investing in assets like these with a goal of generating the stable, long-term flow of funds needed to pay retirees their benefits. The Ontario Municipal Employees Retirement System (OMERS) jointly owns the Detroit River Rail Tunnel with Canadian Pacific Railway, while Ontario Teachers' Pension Plan owns a piece of Northumbrian Water Group, a water utility in Britain, and the Canada Pension Plan has an investment in Transelec, an electrical utility in Chile. It's not feasible for individuals to buy their own bridges and tunnels, but that doesn't mean they can't put infrastructure to work.

Through a growing number of mutual funds, closed-end funds and exchange-traded funds, you can buy into portfolios of global companies that own and operate everything from airports to utilities providing electricity and natural gas. An example is the Claymore Global Infrastructure ETF (CIF-TSX) which holds

Canadian, U.S. and international companies. There's also an infrastructure income trust listed on the Toronto Stock Exchange, Macquarie Power & Infrastructure Income Fund (MPT.UN–TSX), which operates several power-generating plants and a chain of Ontario retirement homes called Leisureworld (they refer to this latter type of investment as "social infrastructure").

The benefits of investing in infrastructure go beyond the reliable returns of the underlying assets. Bridges, highways, tunnels and the like are considered a hedge against inflation because the revenues produced tend to rise along with the cost of living.

2. Water

The basic argument for investing in water is scarcity, starting with the fact that just 2.5 per cent of the world's water is fresh. And yet, the investment dealer Goldman Sachs says consumption of fresh H_2O is doubling every twenty years. The World Water Council says that North Americans use about 350 litres of water a day on a per capita basis in residential areas, compared with 200 litres in Europe and 10 to 20 litres in sub-Saharan Africa. Meanwhile, the American Water Works Association has reported that much of the water network in the United States will need to be replaced in the next thirty years, and the estimated cost of replacing old pipes comes in between $280 billion and $400 billion (both figures in U.S. dollars).

There's a clear case to be made for water as a scare resource worth investing in, and the investment community has agreed. As of mid-2009, there were five ETFs focusing on indexes of water-related stocks. The Canadian Imperial Bank of Commerce has issued a couple of series of principal-protected notes that invest in water stocks, and there's also a mutual fund in the sector called Criterion Water Infrastructure.

The Criterion fund's attributes are its wide availability, its global diversification and its use of currency hedging, which means investors get the returns of the underlying stocks without distortions caused by currency fluctuations. Fees come in at about 2.55 per cent, which is high in comparison to the water ETFs that are listed on the Toronto and New York stock exchanges.

The PowerShares Water Resources Portfolio, listed on the New York Stock Exchange under the symbol PHO, is among the most popular of the water ETFs. The underlying index for this ETF is the Palisades Water Index, which has top holdings that include the URS Corporation, an engineering firm with expertise in water infrastructure projects; Tetra Tech, a consulting and engineering firm; and Valmont Industries, which makes irrigation equipment. Other water ETFs include the PowerShares Global Water Portfolio (PIO–NYSE), the Claymore S&P Global Water ETF (CWW–TSX), and the First Trust ISE Water Index Fund (FIW–NYSE).

3. Agriculture

Investing in commodity stocks used to mean buying energy, mining and, to a lesser extent, forest-product stocks. But in the great commodity boom of mid-decade, investors learned that fertilizer stocks such as Potash Corporation of Saskatchewan and Agrium were also capable of huge, if impermanent, price gains.

There's more to the agriculture story than fertilizer producers, though. Companies in the business of producing farm equipment and seeds are also in a position to benefit.

The underlying story here is the rising level of affluence in countries like China and India. It's increasing demand for food products, and that in turn is boosting food prices and demand for anything that helps increase food production. Demand for agricultural products has been heightened by a trend in which farmers are growing crops for biofuels like ethanol rather than food. Increases in demand for food are outpacing supply, which in turn has resulted in the kind of food inflation that has been apparent to anyone visiting a grocery store (start with breakfast cereal—prices keep climbing).

All commodity stocks are subject to economic cycles—when growth is strong, there's a big demand for raw materials, and the opposite is true when growth slackens. But agricultural commodities are supported by basic supply-and-demand factors like global population growth and declines in the amount of cultivated land. One commodity-investing enthusiast has said the agricultural story, at its simplest, can be explained as another 600 million people, at minimum, being added over the next ten years to the list of those who have a diet something like what we in the West enjoy.

As with water and infrastructure, there's a growing number of fund products for investors who don't want to pick individual stocks in the agricultural sector. A TSX-listed ETF in this group is the Claymore Global Agriculture ETF (COW-TSE), while a mutual fund option is the Criterion Diversified Commodities Fund (it exposes you to a mix of agricultural and resource-based commodities).

THREE LOW-COST WAYS TO BUY STOCKS

Commissions have always been a big deterrent to buying individual stocks as opposed to funds, even as these costs have come way down in recent years. Here are some ways to buy stocks while keeping commissions to as little as nothing.

1. Dividend Reinvestment Plans (DRIPs)

DRIPs are a silent but deadly effective way to make money in stocks. The concept is simple: instead of receiving the dividends paid by a company in cash, you instruct the company to use your dividends to buy new shares. Say you have 100 shares of Royal Bank of Canada and you get 50 cents per share in quarterly dividends. With the shares trading at, let's say, $50, you could use your dividends to buy an additional share every three months. At the end of the year, you'll own 54 shares of RBC, and the additional cost would be nil.

Yes, DRIPs are quite often a free service. Companies like them because they help broaden their shareholder bases and provide a source of capital. In addition to no-charge DRIPs, some companies offer free share-purchase plans (SPPs), which let you invest a lump sum in new shares. A small number of companies even apply a small discount to their share price when shareholders make use of DRIPs and SPPs.

The drawback with DRIPs is that they are somewhat laborious to set up. To start, you have to buy one or more shares of the company you're interested in through a broker, then request to have them registered in your name and sent to you. Total estimated cost: $50 to $100, assuming you use a low-cost discount broker. Next, you have to contact the investor relations department of your target company (or visit the website) and find out where to obtain a DRIP enrolment form and, if you want, an SPP form as well.

No-cost DRIPs are a tradition in Canada, but one notable exception is the insurance giant Manulife Financial. A few years ago, it introduced a DRIP with a fee of 5 per cent of the reinvested dividends up to $6 per quarter, plus GST (deducted from the dividend), as well as a nominal brokerage commission that was initially set at 4 cents a share. The cost for Manulife's SPP is $15 per purchase plus a brokerage commission.

An easy, and sometimes cheap, alternative way of setting up a DRIP is to ask your broker if it provides DRIP services. Many brokers do this as a perk for clients, and they often charge little or nothing. One major drawback: broker DRIPs usually don't allow you to buy fractional shares, whereas company DRIPs usually do.

Staying in a DRIP for extended periods of time is an effective wealth-building technique because you'll add new shares to your portfolio that will in turn generate dividends that buy more new shares. Ideally, you'll also get the benefit of long-term appreciation in the price of your shares. Before you enroll in a DRIP, however, you need to do some research to ensure you're making a commitment to a quality company. Note that Canadian investors can make use of DRIPs offered by U.S. companies.

QuickSurvey: Essential Websites for DRIPers

Site	Web Address
DRIP Central	dripcentral.com
DRIP Investing Resource Centre*	dripinvesting.org
Stingy Investor	ndir.com

*essential reading for Canadian DRIPers

2. Canadian ShareOwner Investments

ShareOwner Investments has all the qualifications of a proper investment dealer, including membership in the Canadian Investor Protection Fund and the Investment Industry Regulatory Organization of Canada. Where ShareOwner Investments is unique is in its attitude. At ShareOwner, it's all about helping people become successful investors and not about stacking up profits through commissions and fees.

ShareOwner is a limited shop in that it offers clients only 200 or so Canadian and U.S. stocks, almost all of them dividend payers, as well as a few dozen exchange-traded funds. The idea is to give clients a head start in building a profitable long-term investment in stocks. Each of the stocks on the ShareOwner menu has been screened using a process that focuses on companies that have shown consistent revenue and profit growth. Among the names to make the grade are the big banks, Rogers Communications, Suncor Energy, Imperial Oil, Canadian National Railway, Power Corporation of Canada, Manulife Financial, Apple, Google, McDonald's and Walt Disney.

You can place an order for a stock any time at ShareOwner, but the service works best as a platform for making regular investments in a group of pre-selected stocks. You can invest pretty much any amount you want into your group of stocks because ShareOwner allows you to own fractional shares. Commissions start at $9 for buying a single stock and top out at $36 for four or more stocks. If you invested $300 monthly into ten stocks every month, you'd pay $36 monthly. The cost of selling a stock is $19, while the cost of spur-of-the-moment purchases is $29 online or $39 on the phone. There are no minimum account requirements at ShareOwner Investments, and you can invest any amount you want on a regular basis. However, it's suggested that people invest at least $200 to $300 at a time to make the commissions economical.

Given its whole-grain focus on healthy investing, it's no surprise that ShareOwner places a big emphasis on dividend reinvestment plans. No matter how many shares you have, the firm will take your dividends and apply them toward the purchase of new shares at no cost. Own just a tiny holding in a particular company? No problem—ShareOwner will parlay your dividends into fractional shares taken down to four decimal points.

ShareOwner Investments offers regular investment accounts and registered retirement savings accounts with an annual administration fee of $59, and tax-free savings accounts at $50 per year. A non-registered account at this firm would be a perfect way to gradually build an investment portfolio outside your RRSP. For more info, go to: investments.shareowner.com.

3. Low-Cost Discount Brokers

Chapter Five will give you the lowdown on discount brokers, but it's worth reinforcing the point right here that these low-cost investment dealers can make investing in stocks quite economical, even for small accounts. The dominant firms in the discount brokerage sector are owned by banks, and they generally have a base rate of somewhere in the range of $25 to $29 to buy up to 1,000 stocks over the Internet. However, there are some smaller firms that offer better deals.

One firm frugal investors should know about is Questrade, which in recent years has been trying to broaden a customer base that at one time was made up mainly of aggressive stock traders. Today, you can set up an RRSP or regular cash account at Questrade with a minimum of $1,000 and immediately take advantage of a commission of one cent per share, with a minimum charge of $4.95 and a maximum of $9.95. Do you find yourself typically buying just a few hundred shares at a time? Then your commissions could well come in around $5 at Questrade (note: exchange and ECN—or electronic communication network—fees may in some cases add to your final cost).

The overall breadth of services at Questrade doesn't come close to the big boys, mind you. If you don't mind paying higher commissions in exchange for more value added, consider Credential Direct and Qtrade Investor, both of which charge a tick under $20 for small online stock orders (some Qtrade orders will cost an extra $4 and may include exchange fees).

Bank-owned brokers have commissions below $10, but customers only qualify if they trade actively—thirty trades per quarter is a typical threshold—or if they have $50,000 to $100,000 in assets with the firm. Note that some brokers will allow you to group all your family's accounts together to reach the required threshold.

Never pick a broker for the sole reason that it's the cheapest for the kind of trading you're going to do. Chapter Five has a lot more information to help you make an informed choice based on price and other factors.

FOLLOW THE YIELD SIGN: THREE PLACES TO LOOK IN THE STOCK MARKETS FOR YIELDS THAT ARE VERY COMPETITIVE WITH WHAT BONDS AND GICS OFFER

We have lived for the past decade in an era of low interest rates. Over that period, it has been a huge victory for income-seeking investors if they were able to lock in money for five years at 5 per cent annually. A fleeting victory, too. More often, rates on bonds and guaranteed investment certificates have bounced between 2 and 4 per cent for terms of one to five years. With inflation likely to be in the range of 2 to 3 per cent over the long term (or even higher—who knows?), those returns are alarmingly low. Want higher yields? Or course you do. Mind higher risk? If the answer is no, then read on.

1. Blue-Chip Dividend Stocks

In normal times, expect dividend yields from 1 per cent to as much as 5 per cent from companies listed on the Canadian and U.S. stock markets. When the stock markets fall as they did in 2008–09, yields for the shares of well established companies can climb as high as 8 to 12 per cent (note: such high yields are a strong—not infallible—signal that a dividend cut may is imminent). Dividend yield is the return you get from the quarterly cash payouts from a company. If you buy a stock for $10 and receive 48 cents in dividends on an annual basis, your stock can be said to have a yield of 4.8 per cent.

A dividend yield of 4.8 per cent can actually be worth more than a GIC or bond with that same return. The reason is that dividends, when received in a non-registered account are taxed with a much lighter hand by the Canada Revenue Agency. In 2009, an Ontario resident making $85,000 a year would pay a marginal tax rate of 43.4 per cent on interest income (treated like any other type of income) and 18.7 per cent on dividends from big corporations.

Dividends are not as secure as interest paid by a bond or GIC. A struggling company can reduce or suspend its dividends to conserve cash, and that is in fact what happened with several of those high-yielding stocks back in 2008–09. For example, Torstar had a yield of about 11.5 per cent in the early going in 2009, then halved its dividend after reporting a quarterly loss of $211 million. Meanwhile, a company would have to be in catastrophically bad shape to stop paying bond interest. GICs, of course, are guaranteed as long as the financial institution issuing them is around (and if it collapses, there are various deposit insurance plans).

The counterbalance to the extra risk component in dividends is the fact that the amount of quarterly cash paid out by premier companies tend to rise over time. Bonds and GICs lock in the amount of interest you get, but a strong dividend-paying blue-chip company could easily boost its dividends by an annual average of, say 5 to 10 per cent or more. Earlier in this chapter, you'll find some suggestions for dividend growth stocks to investigate.

2. Preferred Shares

Preferred shares used to be a widows-and-orphans kind of investment because they paid dividends but never did much price-wise.
In the financial market chaos of 2008–09, however, preferred
shares got lumped in with everything else and suffered a beating
that left many conservative investors cringing at their losses.

It's important to note that the vast majority of these preferred
shares never stopped doing what they were supposed to do,
which is pay a handsome stream of tax-advantaged dividends
(a notable exception was Nortel Networks, which suspended
preferred dividends in fall 2008, a few months before seeking
bankruptcy protection). Still, the price declines in these nor-
mally stable shares were alarming, and many investors dumped
their holdings. The net result: preferred shares became even
more attractive as a way to generate dividend income. How so?
The background here is that a stock's dividend yield rises as the
price declines. So whereas a preferred share issued by some of
the big banks might have had a yield of 4.5 per cent in early
2007, by early 2009 the yield had soared as high as 7 per cent
as a result of a falling share price.

Yes, these bank-preferred shares got riskier as a result of the
instability in the global banking system and the slowing of the
economy. But holders of preferred shares receive, well, prefer-
ential treatment from a company. Dividends on regular
common shares may have to be cut or suspended altogether,
but preferred shares will be paid their full allotment unless
financial stresses are acute. In the investor hierarchy, common
shareholders are at the bottom, preferred shareholders rank
higher and bondholders are at the top.

Preferred shares are generally issued at a price of $25, but they can easily dip below that if the issuing company hits a rough patch or if interest rates start to rise (like bonds, preferred shares lose value when rates rise, and vice versa). There are two ways to benefit from owning preferred shares that trade below $25. One is through a rebound in the fortunes of the issuing company that causes both its common and preferred shares to rise. Another is through a redemption of the shares. Companies issuing preferred shares may redeem those shares on set dates, and the price of redemption is usually $25.

QuickSurvey1: Some Useful Bits of Preferred-Share Jargon

Perpetuals: Preferred shares with no set redemption date.

Retractable: There's a set redemption date for the shares.

Floating rate: Instead of paying a fixed dividend, these shares have a payout pegged to a recognized benchmark like the major banks' prime rate.

Cumulative: If dividends are suspended, a company must pay back all dividends owing when it resumes the quarterly payout.

QuickSurvey2: A Few Quick and Easy Ways to Add Preferred Shares to Your Portfolio

Fund	MER (%)	Type
Omega Preferred Equity	1.41	Mutual Fund
Claymore S&P/TSX CDN Preferred Share ETF (CPD–TSX)	0.45	ETF
PowerShares Preferred Portfolio ETF (PGX–NYSE)	0.50	ETF
iShares S&P U.S. Preferred Stock Index ETF (PFF–NYSE)	0.48	ETF

3. Income Trusts

It's true that trusts are headed into the great unknown as we approach the 2011 introduction of a federal tax that will reduce the amount of money they have available to payout to shareholders every month or quarter. These cash distributions are, after all, the reason to own an income trust. Whereas a traditional corporation will retain its earnings for future growth and perhaps shovel some out as dividends, trusts pay almost all profits out to shareholders, who happily own them in order to receive yields that have ranged from 5 to 12 per cent or more. That was the story on trusts up until the federal government announced the new tax on a fateful Halloween night in 2006.

Since then, trusts have continued to operate, but in an environment of uncertainty. Some have converted themselves back into corporations, and some have found buyers. But many continue to live on pretty much as they always have, making money and then distributing it to investors. Let's be clear here: buying trusts is a risky thing to do in the lead-up to 2011. The danger is that, one way or another, the new trust tax will cause a trust you own to cut back on the amount of cash it distributes. If that happens, you can bank on a large decline in its share price. This can happen even when a trust converts itself into a dividend-paying corporation. The dividends are typically much lower than the old cash distributions, and that usually causes the share price to fall.

Trusts aren't off limits as we head into 2011, however. There are some with strong businesses that are, in theory, capable of growing sufficiently to cover off the amount of the trust tax and still maintain current cash distributions.

QuickSurvey: Four Income Trusts with a Future

Analyst Harry Levant of IncomeTrustResearch.com has been following the trust world for years and years, which is why I asked him for a list of four income trusts he believes will be able to maintain their current income flow to investors after the new trust tax takes effect in 2011. Here are the names he came up with.

1. A&W Revenue Royalties Income Fund (AW.UN):

The venerable old A&W burger chain seems impervious to changing trends and fashions, even while other fast-food income trusts have their problems at times.

2. Bell Aliant Regional Communications Income Fund (BA.UN):

One of North America's largest regional providers of telecom services. A phone utility would seem an ideal business for the income trust structure.

3. Morguard REIT (MRT.UN):

A diversified real estate investment trust—most of the assets are malls and other retail outlets, but offices and industrial properties are part of the mix as well.

4. Vermilion Energy Trust (VET.UN):

A very well-run energy trust that is unusual in having some international exposure and a sterling record for maintaining steady distributions.

FIGHTING THE BEAR, PART I: FIVE LESSONS TAUGHT
BY THE GREAT STOCK MARKET MELTDOWN OF 2008-09

The bright side of the stunning stock market plunge that trauma-tized investors all over the world in the late summer of 2008? Well, the conditions could quite possibly be the worst you'll ever see on the markets. Share prices fall hard every so often—that's as much a part of investing in stocks as those great years of double-digit gains. But 2008 was special, if that's the word. The combination of a breakdown in the global financial system and the onset of a global recession smashed global stock indexes so mightily that investors who at one point in the year were looking at tidy gains suddenly found they were down 20, 30 and even 40 per cent. Here are some lessons learned in this debacle that will serve you well when the stock market plunges the next time.

1. Take profits or rebalance.

When the Canadian stock market peaked in June 2008, more than a few Canadian equity funds were riding a wave that had carried them to one-year gains of 10 to 25 per cent or more. By mid-October, many of these same funds had been utterly dev-astated. In some cases, investors were looking at thirty-day losses of 20-odd per cent. The lesson here is that a portfolio of stocks or equity funds needs to be carefully tended. Complacency kills.

The background to the market debacle of fall 2008 was that the Canadian stock market was coming off five straight years of good gains. That's an exceptional run, and investors should have been on guard for a pullback. How should they have prepared? Not by selling all their stocks or equity funds (who knows, the markets could have kept rising for a while longer), but rather by trimming their exposure to securities that had surged in price. This is called taking profits, and it's something that investors can be loath to do when they're on a winning streak.

A good guideline for profit-taking is to go back to the asset allocation plan, or blueprint, you used when assembling your portfolio. Maybe you figured on 30 per cent exposure to bonds and 70 per cent to stocks, then watched as your equity funds grew to the point where they accounted for 85 per cent of your portfolio. The aggressive approach here would be to let that oversized equity weighting ride. The smart approach would be to sell some of your equity funds and use the proceeds to get your bond holdings back up to 30 per cent.

Rebalancing is something you should look at doing every year at a bare minimum. In fast-rising markets, it wouldn't hurt to take a look at your portfolio every three to six months to ensure everything's still in balance. If you're concerned about losing out on potential gains by rebalancing, look at it this way: you can judiciously take profits yourself, or you can let a bear market do the work for you.

2. Own bonds or GICs.

I have heard more than a few people with top financial credentials tell me they don't own bonds. Their explanation is that in this era of low interest rates, it simply doesn't pay to own them. They feel it's a smarter play to put all their money in the stock markets, while recognizing the greater level of volatility. "Volatility"—that's a word people in the investing industry often use as a euphemism for losing money. It's inevitable that you'll face losses at some point if you invest in stocks. But by keeping some money in bonds or GICs—what investing types call fixed income—you can limit the damage.

The benchmark stock index for Canada, the S&P/TSX composite, fell 33 per cent in 2008 while the benchmark bond index, the DEX Universe Bond Index, gained 6.4 per cent. With 100-per-cent exposure to Canadian stocks, your loss would, of course, have been 33 per cent. With 20 per cent in bonds, your portfolio loss would have been 25.1 per cent. With 50 per cent in bonds, your loss would have been just (*just!*)13.3 per cent.

It's quite possible that a portfolio of pure stocks will outperform a balanced portfolio over a long period of time. But to reap the benefit of an all-stocks approach, you need to be able to shrug off the potential for the kind of stunning losses we saw in 2008 and look ahead to the next bull market. For lots of investors, this is flat-out impossible. They simply can't hack it when their stock portfolio falls 40 per cent in value. Either they sell, or they eat themselves up with worry.

This brings us back to bonds and GICs. In a hard-charging bull market, they're excess baggage in a portfolio. But in a down market, they're a life preserver. We saw that in 2008 and we'll see it again.

3. Don't expect the manager of your equity funds to protect you.
In retrospect, it seems obvious that the stock market was ripe for a fall in mid-2008. The markets were rising, but shaky as a result of the growing global financial crisis. Commodity prices were soaring and stocks in the sector had soared to heights that seemed to reflect unwarranted optimism about the global

appetite for oil, metals and fertilizers. How did the managers of the country's mutual funds size up this environment?

For many, the attitude can best be summed up as "full steam ahead." These guys rolled right into the market storm of fall 2008 and had their butts handed to them. Their clients—investors like you—paid the price. The S&P/TSX composite index lost 33 per cent in 2008, and almost two-thirds of Canadian equity funds did worse than that. The lesson here is that investing professionals cannot be counted on to protect investors from sharp downward turns in the market.

Back in 2000, we saw the large number of mainstream Canadian equity funds that had taken too-large positions in Nortel Networks. In 2008, too many funds got overinvolved with high flyers like Potash Corporation of Saskatchewan, Research in Motion and a host of mining and energy names. When these stocks fell back to earth, the funds that held them were punished.

To be fair, quite a few Canadian equity funds foresaw the commodity reversal and cut their exposure down to minimal levels. They also loaded up on conservative stocks that had not benefited from the market run-up. Yet even these funds were manhandled by the market in 2008. For example, the very well-run CI Harbour Fund lost 24.5 per cent.

Managers of U.S. and global equity funds were no better at protecting their clients from the bear market of 2008. Of the ten largest global equity funds as measured by assets, eight lost more than the benchmark MSCI World Index, as measured in Canadian dollars. Of the ten largest U.S. equity funds, five lost more than the S&P 500 index in Canadian dollars. Look, I'm a believer in mutual funds as a primary investing vehicle of the masses. But it's important not to expect too much from the women and men running these funds. Some of them will make you a good buck over the long term, but in a wicked bear market you can't count on them to provide much of a shield.

4. Global diversification won't protect you.

We've already covered how one type of diversification—mixing bonds or GICs in with your stock holdings—is essential. But there's another type of diversification that turned out to be a resounding failure in the market plunge of 2008. We're talking here about global diversification, which typically means owning U.S. and/or global equity funds, exchange-traded funds or stocks.

You think the countries of the world can't get together on anything? Forget about the squabbling at the United Nations and take a look at global stock markets. They *all* got sliced and diced in 2008. A typical trading day during the market unravelling of October 2008: big market declines in the Far East, followed by big market declines in Europe and then the same in North America. The benefit of global exposure: nil.

Do not read this as a condemnation of global diversification, or as a call to buy Canadian and ignore the other 97 per cent or so of the world's stock markets. While it's sensible to keep a major portion of your holdings in Canada, it's basic common sense to invest in pivotal markets like the United States, Europe and the Far East. There's simply too much happening there to turn your back and look only at the resource-dominated Canadian market.

You have to be realistic about global diversification, though. When a global financial trauma on the order of 2008 occurs, no place is safe.

QuickSurvey: How Global Stock Markets All Got Massacred Together in 2008

Stock Index	% Decline in 2008*
S&P/TSX Composite	33
S&P 500	21.2
MSCI Europe Australasia Far East (EAFE)	29.2
MSCI World	25.8

*These returns include dividends and are expressed in Canadian-dollar terms.

5. Keep cash in your portfolio.

"Cash" is a catch-all phrase to describe funds in your investment or RRSP account that are either left uninvested or put into safe, easily sold things like money market funds, Treasury Bills, Canada Savings Bonds and cashable guaranteed investment certificates. In bull markets, especially in this era of low interest rates, cash is trash. But in a bear market, as the old cliché goes, cash is king because it's safe and secure.

There's no standard rule for setting the percentage of your portfolio that should be invested in cash, but a weighting of 2 to 5 per cent seems like a good minimum for young, fairly aggressive investors. Increase your cash weighting as you get closer to retirement so that you have something like three years' worth of expenses held in cash or liquid investments by the time your registered retirement savings plan is converted into a registered retirement income fund (RRIF).

Seniors were reminded of the importance of this rule in 2008 when some had to sell off hard-hit stocks and equity funds to come up with money for the annual mandatory minimum

RRIF withdrawal set out by the federal government. A solid cash component in an RRIF portfolio gives you something to draw upon should you take a big loss in your investments that are exposed to the stock market.

Younger investors can use cash to capitalize on buying opportunities as they arise in stocks or bonds. True, cash will act as a drag on returns in good times. But you'll be thankful for it in a severe market downturn like 2008 because it will be impervious to falling share prices.

FIGHTING THE BEAR, PART II: A FEW THINGS THAT WORKED WHEN EVERYTHING ELSE WENT SOUTH

Investments that hold up well in bad times are described as being defensive. But some types of investments play defence better than others. Here are a few that hung tough when the financial markets seemed almost to be disintegrating back in 2008.

1. Government Bonds and Treasury Bills

Never mind what they tell you about *bonds* offering a good shelter from stormy markets. It's government bonds they mean here. Corporate bonds are a big part of the fixed-income market as well, but they can be twitchy in a bear market, just like stocks (don't even think about high-yield bonds . . . they're the riskiest end of the corporate bond market). Government bonds are different. They have the backing of the federal or provincial governments and that's as close to risk-free as you get.

In recent years, bonds have offered returns that any sane investor would think of as disappointing. But when the stock markets are melting like an ice cube in July, it feels pretty darn good to own bonds that keep paying you interest.

2. Short-term Bond Funds

This sub-variant in the bond fund family primarily holds government-issued debt maturing in one to five years. When things get really hairy in financial markets, investors don't like to make long-term bets. That's why short-term bonds are favoured over their longer-term counterparts. While the stock markets plunged in 2008, all-inclusive Canadian fixed-income mutual funds made 2.9 per cent on average. Short-term bond funds did better, with an average return of 4.9 per cent. Short-term bonds also pay less than longer-term bonds, but their stability in turbulent markets more than makes up for it.

Short-term bond funds are quite common in the mutual fund world. A better option is one of a pair of exchange-traded funds, the iShares CDN Short Bond Index Fund or the Claymore 1–5 Year Laddered Government Bond ETF. There's more info on both of these ETFs earlier in this chapter.

3. Consumer-Staples Stocks

Come hell, high water or recession, we all gotta eat, right? Don't answer. Let the numbers speak for themselves. The S&P/TSX composite index lost 33 per cent in 2008, but stocks in the consumer-staples sector (selling groceries and other essentials) lost just 8 per cent. By comparison, information technology stocks fell about 50 per cent, financials fell about 39 per cent and energy about 38 per cent.

The roll of honour includes names like the grocery chain

Metro Inc., up almost 40 per cent for 2008. This stock has been an uneven longer-term performer, but was a refuge of choice in 2008. Other consumer-staples stocks to do well in 2008 were George Weston, parent of the Loblaw grocery chain, and Empire Company, which controls the Sobey's supermarket chain as well as a collection of real estate holdings. Weston rose almost 10 per cent in 2008, Empire about 14 per cent.

4. Telecom Stocks

No, the tiny telecom sector didn't stand up to the bear nearly as well as consumer-staples stocks. But the losses turned in by Manitoba Telecom Services, Bell Aliant Regional Communications Income Fund and Telus were a fair bit less than the decline posted by the S&P/TSX composite index.

On a total-return basis, telecom stocks looked even better. Total return measures the change in the share price plus the dividend yield. For a stock like MTS, with a share price decline of about 23 per cent in 2008 and an annual dividend yielding in the 6 to 7 per cent range, the total return for shareholders was a loss of roughly half that of the index. All stocks in the S&P/TSX capped telecommunications index are dividend plays, even Rogers Communications, which fell about 18 per cent in 2008.

What do telecom stocks have going for them in a down market? Mainly, it's their status as near utilities with a locked in customer base that defies economic boom-bust cycles.

5. A *Very Few* Real Estate Investment Trusts

A REIT is a kind of income trust that, every month or quarter, pays out cash generated through rents paid on real estate holdings that range from apartments to offices, industrial complexes and hotels. The broad REIT sector was actually hit quite hard in the financial turmoil of 2007–08, but a few names in the sector emerged comparatively well.

One was Canadian Apartment Properties REIT (CAR.UN-TSX) which owns a portfolio of townhouses and apartments across the country. Whereas REITs with commercial property portfolios were thought to be vulnerable to the economic slowdown that took hold in 2008–09, CAP REIT's portfolio of residential properties was considered less vulnerable to recession. Another survivor was Canadian REIT (REF.UN), which is the country's oldest real estate investment trust, having been first listed on the TSX in the fall of 1993.

Note that some REITs, notably those exposed to office properties, were hit quite hard in the market downturn. An example would be H&R REIT, which fell hard after it ran into difficulties financing a major new development in Calgary.

FOUR

BONDS, GICS AND OTHER CONSERVATIVE STUFF

LET'S BE FRANK ABOUT BONDS, or what the experts like to call "fixed income." They haven't been worth holding since, oh, mid-2000, which is the last time you could have got a return of 6 per cent from a five-year Government of Canada bond. Since then, interest rates have fallen and returns from bonds have been just pitiful. As I write this, the yield on the five-year Canada bond is about 2.5 per cent. Hold bonds in your portfolio? What's the point?

Let's just say it's a mental-health thing. My sense of the investing masses is that an all-stocks, no-bonds approach is a nervous breakdown waiting to happen. Bonds may be a low-return proposition these days, but they still perform the important function of providing a cushion against stock market declines.

So you almost certainly want exposure to bonds in your portfolio, with your exact weighting tied to your age, risk tolerance, investing goals and such. How you go about finding this bond exposure without getting ripped off, exploited and otherwise duped is what this chapter is all about.

FOUR ROTTEN WAYS TO PUT BONDS AND GICS IN YOUR PORTFOLIO

Most likely, you well know how low returns from bonds are these days. This makes it imperative that you don't waste your money on bonds and bond products that are almost sure to underperform. Here are some examples.

1. Bond Funds from Big Mutual Fund Companies

Dang, but big fund companies suck at doing bond funds. Or maybe they don't. It's hard to say exactly how good their bond fund managers are because the funds they run are so overpriced as a rule that it's impossible for investors to get decent results after fees are deducted. I know I've already ranted on this topic in Chapter Two, but it's worth a reprise here. The garden-variety big-company bond fund is your absolute last resort for getting exposure to bonds into your portfolio.

Okay, there are some exceptions. TD Canadian Bond is run by one of the smartest bond fund managers in the country, Satish Rai, and it has done very well over the long term. Trimark Canadian Bond has been a consistently above-average performer, too. But for each of these two funds, it's possible to list dozens of duds from your friends at the country's biggest fund firms.

Notice the use of the term *big* fund companies here. There are numerous smaller fund companies, many of them low-profile independents, who run some pretty decent bond funds. The common characteristics of these companies are (1) a background in running money for pension plans, endowments, foundations and rich people and (2) very low fees, which are a decided edge in with bond funds. Here's a list of five good bond funds in this category:

QuickSurvey: Low-Cost Bond Funds

Fund	MER (%)	10-Year Return (%)	Minimum Investment
PH&N Bond D	0.58	5.5	$5,000
Beutel Goodman Income	0.76	5.7	$10,000
McLean Budden Fixed Income	0.65	5.3	$10,000
Mawer Canadian Bond	0.93	5.1	$5,000
Leith Wheeler Fixed Income	0.80	4.6	$25,000
Category Average	1.65	4.2	

2. Government Bonds Sold by a Discount Broker

Discount brokers live up to their name if you want to trade stocks with commissions that can be as low as $5 to buy or sell. But with bonds, discount brokers are sharks. They just love stripping the meat off unsuspecting retail investors who make the prudent decision to have some super-safe government bonds in their portfolio.

To understand the issue, you first have to know a bit about how bonds work. Bond yields—the annualized return you get on your invested money—move in the opposite direction of bond prices. So if you have to pay a bit more for a bond, you're giving up a little bit of yield, or return. This is precisely how discounters get you when you invest in bonds. They mark up their prices substantially, leaving investors with yields that are bound to disappoint. This applies to bonds of all types, including the federal and provincial government bonds that lots of people gravitate toward because of the safety factor.

Clients of full-service brokers may well find they're able to get a better deal on bonds, particularly if they have a substantial account—well into six figures or more—and a good relationship with their adviser. Meanwhile, clients of discount brokers must wait until the players in the sector decide to compete as hard to lower bond costs and they did with stocks.

3. GICs from Big Financial Institutions

You want big-name stability with your guaranteed investment certificates? The comfort of knowing you own GICs issued by the biggest banks and insurance companies? If so, be prepared to accept much lower returns than you can easily and reliably get from alternative banks, trust companies and credit unions.

GICs are sometimes derided as the investing tool of risk-allergic seniors, but in fact they're a good alternative to bonds for investors of all types (keep reading in this chapter for more info). The thing is, you have to have your head on straight when buying GICs. The security of brand-name financial institutions is not worth the penalty you'll pay in terms of lower returns.

QuickSurvey: A Snapshot Rate Comparison on One Particular Day in 2009

The point of this comparison is to show the variation among financial institutions.

Financial Institution	5-Year GIC Rate (%)
Bank of Montreal	2.20
Bank of Nova Scotia	2.20
Citizens Bank of Canada	2.20
Dundee Bank of Canada	3.45
ING Direct	3.75
ICICI Bank Canada	4.00
Manulife Investments	3.50
Maxa Financial	3.50
President's Choice Financial	2.85
Royal Bank of Canada	2.20
Toronto-Dominion Bank	2.20

4. Canada Savings Bonds

I mention CSBs on the chance that these dinosaurs will continue to avoid extinction for a few more years. Decades ago, when investing was something that only rich people did, CSBs were the foundation of many a small investor's financial portfolio. Of course, it helped that interest rates used to be a lot higher. If you could get, say, 7 per cent from a CSB, what did you need with the stock market or bonds?

In today's low-interest-rate environment, CSBs have one salient characteristic: they consistently pay interest rates that are markedly inferior to what you can get elsewhere. True, CSBs do have the financial backing of the federal government and its top credit rating. But any serious bank, trust company, credit union or insurance company selling guaranteed investment certificates these days is a member of one deposit insurance plan or another.

One last benefit of CSBs, that you can painlessly buy them through payroll deduction, doesn't hold up, either. A better alternative: set up an account with an online bank offering a high-interest savings account—it's a cinch the rates will beat what CSBs are offering—and then arrange to have contributions electronically transferred from the chequing account whenever your paycheque is deposited. Voilà—your own payroll deduction plan.

THREE ALTERNATIVES TO TRADITIONAL BOND FUNDS

No matter how you invest or who your adviser is, there are always alternatives to bond funds. Here are three that are really sweet deals.

1. Bond Index Funds

A good many investors are aware of indexing, which is the strategy of tying your returns to major stock indexes rather than picking individual stocks or buying a mutual fund managed by a professional stock picker. But indexing works with bonds as well, and in fact it works quite effectively.

A big benefit of indexing is low fees. By charging less, an index fund leaves more on the table for investors. This is especially important with bonds, where returns are small to begin with because of low interest rates. We've already seen how high the fees can be with conventional bond funds. Bond index funds are far lower, and the savings flow directly to the investor.

Here's an example. The RBC Canadian Bond Index Fund has a management expense ratio of 0.63 per cent, a little more than a full percentage point less than the average Canadian bond fund. Over the past five years, returns have been above average over almost every single time frame measured by Globeinvestor.com. What's even more impressive is that this fund primarily holds very safe federal government bonds. Corporate bonds offer a little bit higher returns, but also more volatility. Big banks are the main source of bond index funds, so these products are widely available.

QuickSurvey: A Buyer's Guide to Bond Index Funds

Fund	MER (%)	Minimum Investment
CIBC Canadian Bond Index	0.98	$500
CIBC Global Bond Index	1.03	$500
CIBC Cdn Short-Term Bond Index	0.98	$500
RBC Canadian Bond Index	0.63	$1,000
Scotia Canadian Bond Index	0.97	$1,000
TD Canadian Bond Index	0.79	$100

2. Bond ETFs

ETFs, or exchange-traded funds, are index funds that trade like a stock (see Chapter Three for the whole story). The ETF advantage is low fees—vastly lower than conventional mutual funds and significantly lower than index mutual funds. The disadvantage is that you need a brokerage account to buy ETFs.

Got a brokerage account? If not, then consider bond index funds. If yes, then forget about bond index funds and look to bond ETFs, which are pretty much the same thing, only cheaper.

In Canada, there's a wide selection of bond ETFs that let you get exactly the bond coverage you want. Are you especially conservative and leery of volatile investments that bounce around a lot in price? Then consider either the iShares CDN Short Bond Index Fund or the Claymore 1–5 Year Laddered Government Bond ETF. The clever idea behind the Claymore ETF is to reproduce the strategy of bond laddering, in which you divide your money into bonds with terms of one through five years. When a bond matures each year, you reinvest it in a new five-year term. The benefit is that you always have a little money coming due to take advantage of higher interest rates, and you're never forced to reinvest a big chunk of money at once if rates have fallen.

Bond ETFs listed on the Toronto Stock Exchange have you covered if you want to mix some riskier but higher-returning corporate or long-term bonds in your portfolio, and they also provide an option for buying real-return bonds, which offer inflation protection. As mentioned in Chapter Three, one negative with bond ETFs is that they never mature and give you back your principal. Think of them as open-ended bonds.

QuickSurvey: A Buyer's Guide to Canadian Bond ETFs

Fund	MER (%)	Ticker Symbol (TSX)
Claymore 1–5 Year Laddered Government Bond	0.15	CLF
Claymore 1–5 Year Laddered Corporate Bond	0.25	CBO
iShares CDN Short Bond Index	0.25	XSB
iShares CDN Bond Index	0.30	XBB
iShares CDN Long Bond Index	0.35	XLB
iShares CDN Corporate Bond Index	0.40	XCB
iShares CDN Real Return Bond Index	0.35	XRB
iShares CDN Government Bond Index	0.35	XGB

3. GICs from alternative financial institutions

Have you ever heard of Achieva Financial? Probably not. Achieva is in no way a major player in the Canadian financial services sector. In fact, it exists only in a virtual sense because it's an online banking operation run by Winnipeg's Cambrian Credit Union. At this point, the canny investor asks, "Of what possible interest could a no-name outfit like Achieva be to me?" The simple answer has a lot to do with interest.

As I wrote this, Achieva was offering five-year guaranteed investment certificates with an annual rate of 3.75 per cent. According to a very handy source of information on interest rates called Cannex Financial Exchanges (cannex.com), banks were offering posted rates of 2.2 per cent for five-year GICs.

Alternative financial players like Achieva don't just beat the banks. They also typically offer vastly better returns than you can get with government bonds. In fact, there are investment advisers who have pretty much replaced short-term government bonds with higher-yielding GICs from alternative financial institutions. Discount brokers are increasingly selling alternative GICs as well.

Key questions to ask before you hand your money over to any bank, trust company or credit union are: (1) What deposit insurance plan do you belong to? and (2) What are the coverage limits? *All* serious financial institutions will be part of such a plan.

TWO ONLINE RESOURCES THAT HELP BOND INVESTORS GET THE UPPER HAND

To be an informed buyer of bonds and GICs, you need to have a good picture of the interest rate landscape. Here's where to get it.

1. CanadianFixedIncome.ca

There are few investing experiences less satisfying than adding some bonds to a portfolio. You tell your brokerage firm what sort of bond you're looking for, and it tells you what you'll pay. You can't comparison shop without calling around, and who has time for that? You can't go online and see what other investors are willing to buy or sell bonds for because, unlike stocks, there isn't a transparent market for bonds that individuals can tap into. So you buy your bond and hope you're not being exploited too egregiously.

One of your few allies in getting a better handle on bonds is a website called Canadianfixedincome.ca. Run by Perimeter Financial, which operates bond and stock trading networks for institutional investors, this website gives you real-world pricing and yield information for government and corporate bonds. To get a feel for the site, take a look at the pricing and yield data on the bonds listed under Today's Markets. This information covers a selection of widely traded bonds and is updated continuously. Many more bonds are covered in the data box at the bottom of the home page. There are separate listings for Government of Canada bonds, provincials, corporates, strip bonds, municipal bonds and real-return bonds, and each contains a fairly wide sampling of what's out there.

For each bond, you'll find the issuer's name plainly displayed, and the coupon, which is the interest rate on the par value of the bond, or the value you'll get at maturity. Bond prices are displayed in the customary way, which is to show the cost as a percentage of the par value. Some bond issues trade at a premium to their par value, which means you would have to pay somewhat more to buy them than you'd get at maturity. Finally, you'll see the yield for each bond issue, which is your actual return factoring in both the interest you're paid and the price of the bond.

Prices and yields provided for each bond issue should be regarded as wholesale rates applicable to people investing larger amounts than the usual $5,000 minimum. In practical terms, this means investors should expect to pay somewhat higher prices for bonds than those displayed on the website. The markup can be considered a commission charged by a broker for the service of selling the bond.

2. Cannex Financial Exchanges

The Cannex website (Cannex.com) is where you go if you're not satisfied with the yields you can get on bonds and guaranteed investment certificates. Cannex is a supplier of data on financial product, including rates on term deposits, also known as GICs. The firm's website is the quickest and easiest way to canvass pretty much the entire financial sector to see what the best GIC rates are.

As I'm writing this, I see via the aforementioned Canadianfixedincome.ca that a five-year Province of Ontario bond offers a yield of about 2.7 per cent. That's a wholesale rate, remember, so the actual yield an investor gets would likely be somewhat lower. Could an investor do better than that in the GIC market? Let's check with Cannex.com

The quick answer is yes. While five-year GICs from the big banks were yielding in the low 2-per-cent range, the online bank ING Direct was offering 3.75 per cent, as were a few other alternative financial players. Next step: contact your broker or check its website to see if you can buy GICs from these institutions for your investment account. Or you can try dealing with them directly.

Cannex sells its data to customers, but it makes some of it available for free on its website. In addition to GIC rates, you can get no-charge access to returns on high-interest savings accounts and mortgage rates. An alternative source of rate info is the Canoe Money website at money.canoe.ca/rates.

GICS WITH A TASTE OF STOCK MARKET EXPOSURE? SIX REASONS TO SAY NO TO PRINCIPAL-PROTECTED NOTES

Principal-protected notes, or PPNs, are the answer to a question a lot of investors have asked, which is how they can invest in the stock market without that ever-so-disturbing risk of losing money. Savvy investors know that as you tamp down the risk profile of an investment, so do you also limit returns. And yet, PPNs have attracted billions from investors who are betting they can tap into the returns of the stock market with a bank-supplied guarantee that they'll at least get their upfront investment back on maturity. I see the attraction of PPNs, but I still think they're a bad investment. Here's why.

1. The Misunderstood Guarantee, Part 1

With a PPN, you can invest in stocks, stock indexes, mutual funds, hedge funds and commodities with a promise from a major brand-name bank that you'll do no worse than get your money back at the end of a term that is often five years in length. The stock market can certainly be a scary place, but is that any reason to buy an investment that pretends it's a good thing to tie your money up for years and end up with a return of zero?

Even a GIC, the faithful friend of investors panicked by stock market risk, offers a better outcome. In recent years, five-year GICs have offered a bulletproof opportunity to make 3 to 5 per cent annually. And then there's the fact that breaking even on an investment is actually losing money in a real-world sense because of inflation. Bank of Canada data show that the average annual rate of inflation over the past five years was 1.9 per cent. That's enough to have raised the cost of a typical basket of consumer purchases from $5,000 to $5,493 over that period. Yes, you'll get your principal back with a PPN, but that doesn't mean you haven't lost ground.

2. The Misunderstood Guarantee, Part 2

Could there possibly have been a more powerful demonstration of the benefits of PPNs than when the stock markets crashed in 2008? On the surface, PPNs looked like the right product at the right time. That market was plunging, but PPN investors were totally safe. So what's the problem? It's simple: stock markets rebound from crashes, but PPNs may not.

It turns out that when the markets go south, many PPNs experience what's known as a "protection event." In other words, the PPN goes into a survival mode that forgoes all chance of making money in the future in order to deliver on the principal guarantee. The worst part is that investors have to hold until maturity to get their money back. If the protection event happens in the first year of a five-year term, you've got four years of dead money to look forward to.

3. High Fees that Aren't Clearly Disclosed

Unfortunately, issuers of PPNs are not required to meet the exact same disclosure standards as mutual funds, which call for a simple and complete itemizing of all fees and their impact on returns. PPN disclosure requirements have been increased lately, but in general these investments can still unleash a plague of fees that cumulatively undermine your returns.

Be on the lookout for sales commissions of up to 4 per cent or more, which is something in the area of two times the highest commission advisers are charging on mutual funds these days. If you pay an upfront fee to buy a mutual fund, you'll avoid having to pay a redemption fee when you sell. With PPNs, there can also be fees to cash out within a set number of years of buying.

4. Lack of Clarity About Returns

One of the most detestable things about PPNs is the way they prey on unsophisticated investors who are satisfied with being told they'll have exposure to various stock market–related securities without risk of loss. Right, but exactly what kind of exposure? That's the question that PPNs too often skip over.

What you do get is a lot of verbiage that leads you on about the earning potential of the indexes, stocks, funds or whatever your PPN is based on. Sure, those investments sound appealing. The question is, how much will you actually make after the company that built your PPN takes its cut? And how much do the underlying investments have to make in order for your PPN to beat return of a GIC or bond? PPN issuers don't answer these questions. After all, they're selling the idea of safe investing, not telling you the truth about how lame PPN returns can be in some cases.

5. Lack of Liquidity

One of the advantages that PPNs have is that you can sell them prior to maturity on the open market. That's the theory, anyway.

In reality, there are pitfalls that call into question whether you can sell a PPN before maturity on decent terms. First off, some PPN issuers say they will maintain a weekly market, while others offer daily liquidity. Then there's the question of how big a gap there is between what sellers are asking and buyers are willing to pay. A large bid-ask spread cuts into your proceeds the same way as those redemption fees that PPNs also charge in some cases.

6. Overall Sneakiness

Even investment advisers and analysts find PPNs unclear in the way they operate. "They are a nightmare to try to understand," the independent mutual fund analyst Dave Paterson once told me in response to a column I wrote on these investments. "If I am getting frustrated by it, I can only imagine what a typical adviser or client is going through."

TWO WAYS TO GET HIGHER YIELDS THAN GICS AND GOVERNMENT BONDS, THOUGH WITH EXTRA RISK

One of the many lessons of the financial crisis of 2008 was that government bonds and big-bank GICs, with their deposit insurance coverage for up to $100,000, are pretty much worry-free investments. But they're also low-return investments that may not leave you with anything after inflation is considered. The problem in seeking higher returns is that you must incur a higher level of risk. Are you okay with this idea? If so, consider these two ways to get higher returns from a fixed-income investment. Note: They come with a higher level of risk of default, where interest payments are suspended and you don't get your money back at maturity.

1. Investment-Grade Corporate Bonds

Companies raise money to finance their operations in a number of ways, and one of them is by issuing bonds that get bought up by pension funds, insurance companies, mutual funds and individual investors. Corporate bonds pay higher interest rates than government bonds because there's a higher risk of default. If a government is financially strapped, it can always resort to raising taxes. Companies in big trouble can ultimately end up in bankruptcy.

It's possible to invest in corporate bonds and contain the default risk, however. Just stick to investment-grade bonds, which means those that have been given an upper-tier credit score by a bond-rating agency. The higher a bond's rating, the lower the risk and the lower the return. At DBRS, a major Canadian bond rating firm, BBB (low) is the lowest investment-grade rating. If you wanted to give yourself an added margin of safety, you could stick to bonds with ratings of BBB (high), A or even AA.

The risk profile of corporate bonds was evident in the financial crisis that blew up in 2008. While government bonds provided a strong hedge against stock market declines, corporate bonds fell significantly. The reason was concern about how bond-issuing companies would weather the global recession. It's important to remember that bonds are an investment you buy to generate income. As long as those semi-annual interest payments come in on time, the price of the bond is of secondary consideration. That said, it bothers some investors to see their bonds falling hard in price. If this is you, the extra yield from corporate bonds may not be worth it.

QuickSurvey1: How the Yields Varied on Corporate Bonds with Different Investment-Grade Ratings in the First Half of 2009. This is a snapshot in time and not a definitive guide.

Bond	Yield (%)	Rating
HSBC Financial Corp. 4.35% 06-OCT-2011	5.17	A
Telus 5.95% 15-APR-2015	5.15	A (low)
Cdn Natural Resources 4.95% 01-JUN-2015	5.74	BBB (high)
Shaw Communications 7.5% 20-NOV-2013	5.51	BBB (low)

How to read this chart: The company issuing the bond is listed, followed by the coupon rate on the bond. (Coupon means the annual interest rate based on the original price of the bond.) Next comes the date the bond matures. Bond yields reflect a variety of factors, including credit rating, coupon and time until maturity.

QuickSurvey2: Some Quick and Easy Ways to Get Corporate Bonds into Your Portfolio

The iShares CDN Corporate Bond Index Fund (XCB-TSX)

This exchange-traded fund tracks the DEX All Corporate Bond Index, which is what people look to when they want to measure the performance of the broad Canadian corporate bond market. If you invest in this ETF, you have well-diversified exposure to dozens of bonds issued by the big banks and insurance companies, utilities, industrial companies and infrastructure such as airports and highways. The management expense ratio is no great bargain at 0.40 per cent, but this ETF is still an excellent way to mix some higher-yielding corporate bonds in with your safer government bonds or GICs. Interest is paid quarterly. A newer alternative is the Claymore 1–5 Year Laddered Corporate Bond ETF (CBO-T).

The iShares iBoxx $ Investment Grade Corporate Bond Fund (LQD-NYSE)

Think of this ETF as being the U.S. version of the iShares CDN Corporate Bond Index Fund. Holdings have included bonds issued by the likes of Pepsico, Berkshire Hathaway (that's Warren Buffett's holding company), IBM and Johnson & Johnson. Blue-chip quality, in other words. The MER for this ETF is quite reasonable at 0.15 per cent. Note the currency risk with this ETF. If the Canadian dollar rises against the U.S. dollar, your returns will be undercut. If the dollar falls, your returns will be pumped up beyond what the underlying bonds return.

TD Corporate Bond Capital Yield Fund

Here, we have a conventional bond mutual fund that specializes in corporate bonds rather than in government bonds or a mix of government and corporate debt. This fund was knocked around some in the rough markets of 2008, a fact that highlights its unsuitability for people who want their bond funds to provide safety and solidity. Rather, this fund offers a way for investors who don't have access to exchange-traded funds to add the higher yields of corporate bonds to their portfolio. Also consider the PH&N Total Return Bond Fund (the D version is best), which typically keeps more than half of its assets in corporate bonds. The PH&N fund is a true mutual fund bargain, with its MER of 0.58 per cent. The TD fund's MER is 1.58 per cent.

2. High-Yield Bonds

Known in some circles as junk bonds, high-yield bonds are issued by companies that have lower-tier credit ratings and must therefore offer jumbo-sized interest payments to attract investors. If you're a bit leery of corporate bonds because of extra risk, just forget about high-yield bonds.

If you can wrap your head around the idea of bonds with risk levels more comparable to stocks than to government bonds, then high-yield bonds might be worth a look. Watch out if you're holding these bonds in a recession, though. Companies with low credit ratings are less able to weather a financial downturn, so they present a much more tangible default risk than investment-grade corporate bonds, or government bonds.

Remember the BBB (low) rating that was the minimum for investment-grade corporate bonds? Well high-yield bonds are below that. The lower you go, the higher the return and risk profile. The trick is to find the bonds with low ratings, high yields but solid enough businesses to keep default at bay. It's a tough job and one that most individual investors probably shouldn't try. If you see a high-yield bond with a double-digit yield, that's a warning sign that investors are very concerned about default risk.

Another problem in buying high-yield bonds is that many discount brokers don't offer them. Through some bizarre and misguided attempt to protect clients, these brokers confine their offerings to investment-grade bonds. Note that you can buy any rubbish the stock market has to offer through these same brokers.

QuickSurvey: Some Quick and Easy Ways to Get High-Yield Bonds into Your Portfolio

SPDR Barclays Capital High Yield Bond ETF (JNK-NYSE), iShares iBoxx $ High Yield Corporate Bond Fund (HYG-NYSE), PowerShares High Yield Corporate Bond Portfolio (PHB-NYSE)

These are all exchange-traded funds listed on the New York Stock Exchange. Each was absolutely hammered in 2008, with declines coming in around 25 to 35 per cent. At the same time, however, the yields on these ETFs rose as high as 10 to 15 per cent. They're not for risk-averse investors and even risk junkies should limit their exposure. Note the currency risk.

PH&N High Yield Bond

This is one of the best of Canada's not especially dynamic crowd of high-yield mutual funds. The 1.3-per-cent gain for this fund in 2008 was a super performance in the face of market developments that drove some competing funds to double-digit losses. The MER is comparatively low at 0.93 per cent for the D version of this fund, which is meant for do-it-yourself investors.

FIVE

DO-IT-YOURSELF
INVESTING

YOU WOULDN'T PERFORM SURGERY ON YOURSELF, would you? Or defend yourself in court in a major lawsuit, or try to fix the transmission of your car? Of course not. You need experts for that—professionally trained doctors, lawyers, mechanics and whatnot. Is investing the same thing? No way. Despite what investment advisers will tell you, do-it-yourself investing is both sound and sensible.

Now a proviso or two. You need to have a good—not adequate or so-so, but *good*—knowledge of investing, and you need both the time and the inclination to manage your portfolio. If you doubt your ability to run your own money, then don't. Read Chapter Six and find yourself an ace adviser to take care of things for you. If you see yourself as a self-directed investor, or if you're already managing your own portfolio, then this chapter is essential reading.

When I talk about do-it-yourself investing, I mean running your own portfolio through a discount broker, also commonly an online broker because most transactions are made on secure websites. The main job of a discount broker is to execute trades. There's no advice provided and clients are expected to know what they're doing. Your big reward for using a discount broker is the opportunity to pay far less than you would for investments bought through an adviser. But there's a lot more to it than that.

FIVE STRONG REASONS TO USE A DISCOUNT BROKER

Many investors end up with a discount brokerage either because of a bad experience with an investment adviser or a realization that they know enough about investing to manage their own accounts effectively. In fact, there are several benefits to using a discount broker.

1. Lower Fees and Commissions

Discount brokers charge a minimum of $5 at the low end and $29 at the high end for each online trade, depending on how much you have in assets and how often you trade. With $100,000 in total assets at a firm, you're virtually certain to pay just a tick below $10.

Full-service brokers have complicated grids for calculating trading commissions, but it's fair to say that the minimum charge for a stock trade would be something like three times the most expensive discount brokerage commission.

Mutual funds are markedly cheaper at online brokers as well. You can buy and sell a wide variety of funds at no cost, and one broker, RBC Direct Investing, offers a special low-fee version of RBC funds that are meant exclusively for do-it-yourself investors. Questrade, another discounter, offers a service whereby the trailing commissions built into funds (see Chapter Two) are rebated to customers.

Discount brokers are generally cheaper as well when it comes to annual administration fees for registered accounts. Even when they do have onerous fees for these accounts, they waive them when your account grows to levels of $15,000 to $25,000, depending on the firm.

2. A Vast Selection of Investment Choices

A large number of investment advisers are licensed only to sell mutual funds, which means buying blue-chip dividend stocks or government bonds is out of the question. Other advisers shape their menu of investments available to clients using reasons that border on the unethical. Examples would be a focus on mutual funds or wrap programs that pay above-average remuneration to advisers.

When dealing with a discount broker, you can buy pretty much anything—the vast majority of mutual funds; all exchange-traded funds listed on North American exchanges, and all stocks, too; bonds issued by companies and governments; GICs issued by solid big banks and small but feisty alternative banks that offer top rates. Not that you'd want to, but you can also buy such investment-industry refuse as principal-protected notes and wrap accounts from discounters.

Discount brokers make most of their money from stock-trading commissions, but they're happy to sell you pretty much anything to keep you as a client.

3. Useful Resources to Help You Invest Intelligently

Discount brokers have really improved over the past several years in offering tools to help clients make sound investing decisions. The reason is simple: successful investors are happy clients who generate lots of commission and fee revenue.

Many brokers offer financial planning tools that start by helping you get an indication of how much you need to save for retirement. Then, these calculators will help you build a portfolio with an appropriate mix of stocks, bonds and cash. If you're just winging it with your investments, this sort of input can provide a useful reality check.

Most brokers offer some kind of equity research these days, typically analyst reports on specific stocks and sectors. Smart investors use this information as a source of ideas for stocks to buy, and as a second opinion. Fund and bond research is commonly available as well.

4. Convenience

Discount brokerage websites are open 24/7, which means you can conduct research and perform account maintenance any time that's convenient for you. If you need to speak to someone, several firms have live representatives available by phone on evenings and weekends. It's also possible to send secure emails to your broker twenty-four hours a day.

Your ability to buy and sell securities is obviously limited by the hours that financial markets are open. However, you can place orders in off-hours that will be executed when the markets open on the next trading day (be careful when doing this with stocks, especially when the markets are volatile).

5. Satisfaction

Investing should never be recreational, because that leads to mistakes like overtrading. But there's no doubt that many people find it enjoyable and stimulating to manage their own investments.

FIVE KEY CONSIDERATIONS IN CHOOSING A DISCOUNT BROKER

What kind of an investor are you? Do you trade stocks several times a week or once or twice per year? Do you use funds much? Are you looking for research to help you pick stocks? Do you have a big six-figure account or are you a beginner? Some brokers are certainly better than others on the whole, but the best broker for you depends on your personal investing profile. Here are some things to look at to ensure you find the right broker.

1. Costs for Your Type of Account and Trading

First, decide what type of investment will form the foundation of your portfolio. If it's stocks or options, then check a broker's commission chart and see how much you'll pay based on your account size, the volume of trading that you do and the kind of stocks you buy (some firms have different prices for penny stocks versus higher-priced shares). If you do any significant amount of stock trading, check out whether a broker charges ECN (electronic communications network) fees in addition to posted commission rates.

If you prefer mutual funds, then look for a broker that charges nothing to buy or sell funds. If you've got your eye on particular funds, then be sure a broker you're considering offers these products, and that they're sold commission-free.

Those just starting out as do-it-yourself investors should pay particularly close attention to small-account fees and inactivity fees in non-registered accounts, and annual administration fees in RRSP accounts.

2. Resources

A degree of parity has settled into the discount brokerage sector in terms of the tools and research that are offered to clients. But don't just assume the resources a broker offers will be useful to you. If you want research on stocks, for example, check to see what volume of reports is available and from what source. The bank-owned discount firms excel here because they typically offer equity research from their in-house full-service brokers.

Discount brokerage clients don't tend to use financial planning tools much, but they should. Most brokers offer them—some are quite useful, while others are too basic to be of any value.

3. Trading Platform

If you plan to trade stocks on a regular basis, pay close attention to the trading platform a broker offers, because it's going to be pivotal. The physical layout of the trading screen is important, and you can get a glimpse of it at most brokers by visiting their public website and taking a guided tour of the secure website for clients.

Serious traders will look for features like being able to make multiple trades at once, and they'll also want Level II quotes, which offer a higher level of detail than the typical stock quote.

4. Who's Running the Firm?

Any reputable broker will be a member of the Canadian

Investor Protection Fund (CIPF), which protects client assets in brokerage accounts for up to $1 million. So there's no need to worry about a broker going bankrupt and taking your account with it.

Still, having your brokerage go under would be a huge hassle that could tie your money up when you need access to it. That's why it's worth taking a look at who owns a brokerage firm and how long it's been in business. This may make it seem that I favour bank-owned firms over low-profile independent brokers, but that's not the case. I just believe investors should verify who they're dealing with before opening an account.

5. Getting Money In and Out of Your Account

This is a comparatively small matter, but one that will make life easier for you as a discount brokerage client. Whether you have a cash account or a registered account, you're going to want to get money into your account—and maybe out as well. If you deal with a broker owned by your bank, this is easy. You'll be able to move your money electronically between your brokerage and bank accounts with ease.

If you deal with an independent broker, or one owned by a bank that you don't otherwise deal with, then check to see if the firm is listed as a bill payee on your online banking website. If it is, you can get money into your account in the same way as you pay a bill online. Alternatively, see if a broker offers electronic money transfers between your brokerage account and a chequing account at any old financial institution (you'll have to submit a void cheque to make this work).

THREE TOP DISCOUNT BROKERS YOU SHOULD CONSIDER USING

For more than a decade, I've been compiling an annual ranking of discount brokers for *The Globe and Mail.* There have been different winners over the years, but some names have consistently been among the top contenders because of their emphasis on continual improvements and maintaining an overall level of good service. Let's introduce you to these brokers, which are listed alphabetically.

1. BMO InvestorLine (bmoinvestorline.com)

This division of Bank of Montreal has long struck me as one of the most thoughtfully designed of the thirteen or so discount brokers that Canadians have to choose from. Clearly, the people running InvestorLine keep asking themselves, "What can we do to help clients be successful investors?"

InvestorLine was one of the first brokers to offer online bond trading, to offer a serious asset allocation tool to help clients design sound portfolios, to present personalized rate of returns and to offer customized instant portfolios corresponding to a client's own particular needs. Another InvestorLine innovation is an online message centre called MyLink that offers reminders to clients about portfolio-maintenance matters like maturing bonds and GICs, while also allowing clients to contact InvestorLine staff to ask questions.

InvestorLine's fees could be lower, notably in the buying and selling of some mutual funds, and it doesn't throw around as much equity research as some of its competitors. But it's a discount brokerage that really seems to care about giving its clients what they need to prosper.

2. Qtrade Investor (qtrade.ca)

This low-profile Vancouver-based outfit has been a consistent top performer in the *Globe*'s annual discount brokerage ranking. How is it that Qtrade has beaten out competitors that are run by the country's biggest and richest banks? Simple—Qtrade is a shrewd imitator of the best practices of its competitors.

Whereas the bank-owned discount brokers can take years to make improvements, Qtrade is constantly matching the innovations in the industry. When commissions were falling, Qtrade was there. When security guarantees against losses due to fraud were being introduced, Qtrade was there, too. Same story when some brokers began to get serious about providing a proper level of data to show clients how their accounts were performing. Qtrade has also built a very good trading platform, and a shelf of investing tools that should satisfy most investors.

What Qtrade doesn't offer is the confidence-inspiring backing of a major bank. In fact, it's privately owned and gets most of its customers by partnering with credit unions and financial advice firms. Qtrade probably won't come to you with flashy marketing, so it's up to you to check it out yourself.

3. TD Waterhouse (tdwaterhouse.ca)

TD Waterhouse dominates online trading in Canada, and that's because it jumped into the business around the time of an Ontario Securities Commission ruling in 1983 opened the way for discount brokers to compete with full-service investment dealers. There's nothing flashy or especially innovative about TD Waterhouse, but it does offer everything a middle-of-the-road investor needs to be successful, including a very good selection of resources for researching stocks and funds.

A perk of dealing with TD Waterhouse is that you can invest in a series of index mutual funds offered by the TD family that can only be purchased online. This "e-Series" offers the lowest management expense ratios of any index fund and represents a good alternative to exchange-traded funds for investors who want to make regular monthly purchases. The advantage of using an index fund for this purpose is that you don't have to pay any purchase commissions, and you get automatic reinvestment of dividends.

QuickSurvey: A Look at the Other Online Brokers

CIBC Investor's Edge (investorsedge.cibc.com): A middling broker that offers a good library of analyst reports on stocks.

Credential Direct (credentialdirect.com): The credit union movement's in-house broker, Credential has low fees and is quite a decent service overall.

Disnat (disnat.com): Operated by Caisse Desjardins, the giant Quebec credit union, Disnat has steadily been improving a service that in past years was neglected.

HSBC InvestDirect (investdirect.hsbc.ca): Run by HSBC, a global bank based in the United Kingdom, this broker is worth a look if you want to trade stocks on global exchanges outside North America.

National Bank Direct Brokerage (nbdb.ca): An okay broker if you're a client of National Bank.

Questrade (questrade.com): A small independent firm with trading commissions that start as low as $4.95, no matter how often you trade or how much you have in your account. Also the first to allow clients to hold U.S. dollars in their registered accounts.

RBC Direct Investing (rbcdirectinvesting.com): Royal Bank of Canada has put some money into improving its online brokerage arm, and the results will especially be appreciated by people looking for tools and resources to help them choose stocks.

Scotia iTrade (scotiaitrade.com): This firm was what resulted when Bank of Nova Scotia absorbed the former E*Trade Canada, which was a low-fee leader in Canadian online investing. As of early 2009, Scotiabank's ScotiaMcLeod Direct Investing was still operating, and it was unclear what the future held for it.

TradeFreedom (tradefreedom.com): A Scotiabank-owned online investing option for aggressive traders that, in early 2009, had an uncertain future as a result of the takeover of E*Trade Canada.

FIVE THINGS YOU DON'T NEED TO WORRY ABOUT IF YOU USE A DISCOUNT BROKER

Discount brokers are virtual operations, which is to say that you use their services not at bricks-and-mortar branches but over the Internet or by telephone. Does that idea make you feel some trepidation? Make no apologies if the answer is yes. I worry a lot more about investors who are complacent and unquestioning than I do about the ones who might have the following concerns.

1. Security

Don't get the wrong idea here. There have been cases of online brokerage accounts being breached, and unauthorized trading has occurred in client accounts. It's rare, though, and it's similarly rare that you'll be held responsible if you took the proper precautions to keep your password and user name safe. Never disclose either to anyone, and be especially wary about those phony, but somewhat official-looking phishing emails that try to get you to log into your brokerage account (scammers can get at your personal information if you do). Fact: no broker or bank or any other financial company will *ever* contact you by email and ask that you log into your account for one reason or another.

And what if something does go wrong in your account? Almost all online brokers now offer a security guarantee that offers 100 per cent protection against losses due to an intrusion into your account, provided you kept your password and user ID secret. Another key level of security: all brokers use heavy-duty encryption that scrambles your personal data when it's in transit between your computer and your broker's computer.

2. Having to Buy 100 Shares of a Stock

One of the biggest all-time investing misconceptions is that you have to buy stocks in board lots of 100. Wrong. The truth is that you can buy as many or as few shares of a company as you choose when using a discount broker. The economics of buying a few shares of a company may look dicey if you're paying $29 for the transaction, but no one from your brokerage firm is going to call you up and laugh at you.

Some brokers may flash a message on their online stock order screens saying that you may not get the best possible price for your purchase if you buy what's known as an odd lot. But if you're investing in a stock that generates a lot of trading, then you shouldn't have a problem. A real-world example of buying a single share: I've heard of lots of people who own just one Class B share of Berkshire Hathaway, billionaire Warren Buffett's holding company. The shares traded around $2,800 (U.S.) when this book was written.

3. Feeling Intimidated

Placing your first online order for stocks is exhilarating but also a little intimidating because you're going to feel like a new and largely insignificant player in a universe of fast-moving money. Get over that feeling. Trading stocks is easy, provided you do a little preparation to master some terms that may be unfamiliar.

Many discount brokers provide online tutorials or glossaries that help you understand the small number of technical terms involved in buying and selling stocks, and one firm, RBC Direct Investing, had just introduced practice accounts for new clients who want to learn the ropes using imaginary money. Here are three need-to-know points about online stock trading:

Get the details right. Be sure to use the correct stock symbol, specify the correct market on which it trades (several stocks are listed on both Canadian and U.S. exchanges) and indicate the correct account. You could, for example, have a margin account, an RRSP account and an RESP account with the same broker. It's surprisingly easy to trade in the wrong account by accident.

Limit orders are best. With a limit order, you specify the maximum you're willing to pay for a stock or the minimum you're willing to accept as a seller. The alternative is a market order, where you accept whatever price your broker gets for you. Limit orders simply give you more control, although market orders may be filled faster and, with some brokers, at a slightly cheaper cost.

Double-check your trades. After submitting your order, you'll jump to a confirmation screen that allows you to take once last look at it before it's executed by your broker. Check all the details once more and then decide whether to submit the order, change it or kill it. The confirmation screen affords an opportunity for sober second thought—take advantage.

4. Not Being Able to Keep Your Portfolio Simple or Conservative

You do *not* have to be a stock jock to be an effective do-it-yourself investor. In fact, there's a good argument to be made for using a discount broker if you simply want to invest in mutual funds and guaranteed investment certificates. Almost all discount brokers sell thousands of different mutual funds from all major fund companies without any buy-or-sell commissions (short-term trading fees may apply if you buy and sell within a few months), and many offer GICs from a wide array of financial institutions, including the ones with the highest rates.

It's worth noting that a couple of discount brokers, TD Waterhouse and CIBC Investor's Edge, have RRSP accounts with cut-rate annual administration fees for clients with small accounts that are invested strictly in funds and GICs or bonds.

An advantage of having a funds-and-GICs account at a discount broker is that you can graduate to buying individual stocks and bonds when or if you want to.

5. Not Having Any Help

The whole concept of the discount broker is to cut advice completely out of the equation and thereby offer lower commissions and fees than full-service investment dealers. In fact, a discount broker is prohibited by securities industry regulations from advising clients about what stocks, bonds, funds and such to buy or sell. So don't bother asking. What you can ask for is basic help in matters like making a stock trade, placing an order for a bond or guaranteed investment certificate or choosing mutual funds.

The bigger bank-owned brokers are best at this. They're well aware that some of their customers are migrating to do-it-yourself channels and may lack confidence and savvy. That's why these firms often have knowledgeable people to answer general questions and more specialized staff on their stock, bond and mutual fund desks to answer specific queries. These people won't tell you what to buy, but they can make sure you have all possible information in hand to make your own decision. Here's a suggestion if you're a novice discount brokerage client calling in with a question: explain right off the top you're a beginner who needs some basic information. Ask to have jargon words explained if you don't understand them and don't try to bluff your way through. Ignorance is almost always punished in the game of investing.

REALITY CHECK: FOUR THINGS DISCOUNT BROKERS DO BADLY

Discount brokers provide a generally sound and valuable service, but let's be mindful of their weaknesses.

1. Delivering Reliable Access to Hyperactive Stock Markets

One of the key lessons of the last two bear markets for stocks—we're talking about 2001–02 and 2008–09 here—is that discount brokers can't handle the crush when trading volumes go through the ceiling. Let's set the scene: it's 9:30 a.m. on a Monday, the stock markets are rallying after a brutal week and you want to place a trade through your discount brokerage account. You log into your account and . . . nothing. Your broker's website is so overloaded that you can't log in at all.

Or maybe you get in but can't get the stock-trading page to load properly. Or maybe you're able to place your stock order and submit it, but then you can't get any confirmation that the order was received or executed. This experience isn't a given when the markets are crazy, but you have to be prepared for it. A rule of thumb is to avoid, if at all possible, placing trades around the 9:30 a.m. market open and the 4 p.m. market close. Some investors have a trick for avoiding the market open crush—they log into their broker's website at, say 9 a.m., and then periodically refresh the screen or move around in the website so as not to have their session timed out. Then, when the market opens, they're ready to go. The only problem is that sometimes a busy broker's website will spontaneously become unavailable because of heavy traffic. One other tip is not to rely on your broker's live agents to pick up the slack left by an unusable website. The queue for waiting to speak with a trader on the phone can last up to an hour in busy times.

2. Offering Fair Pricing on Bonds

It isn't just me saying that discount brokers are pirates when it comes to selling bonds to clients. Several years ago, the retired former head of bonds for one of the country's largest mutual fund families contacted me to express his amazement at how discount brokers were ripping off clients buying bonds. This former fund honcho had set up his own discount brokerage account and was buying some bonds. The prices he was quoted were so much higher than he was used to as a professional that he had to speak out.

Here's why you should care about high bond prices. Bond prices and bond yields move inversely, which is to say that a higher price will mean a reduced yield. In this era of low interest rates, investors absolutely have to fight for every bit of extra yield they can get. That means getting the price they pay for bonds as low as possible.

The first reason why this is so hard to do is the fact that the market for bonds is not like it is for stocks, where there's a sort of open auction process that permits buyers and sellers to know exactly what each other is willing to pay or accept. With bonds, you ask your broker for a price and you have to live with what you're told. There's no mechanism for individual investors to see what other investors and other dealers are willing to offer them in terms of bond pricing.

If you're a client of a full-service investment dealer, have a good relationship with your adviser and you're a valued client (translation: you have a significant account in the high six figures), then you may be able to negotiate slightly improved bond prices. By all means, try this if you're a discount brokerage client with a big account. If you have a smaller account, you have zero power to get better bond prices. Your preferred option: see what your broker is offering in terms of GICs from alternative banks, trust companies and credit unions that have to offer top rates to attract clients.

3. Offering a Good Selection of Bonds

Here's another example of how retail investors suffer because the bond market isn't as open as the stock market. If you want to buy a stock listed on a major North American stock exchange, any broker can sell it to you. Not so with bonds.

Check the bond inventories of a few different online brokers and you'll find some overlap, but also a lot of names that crop up here but not there. You want a three-year corporate bond with a rating of A or maybe BBB (high)? Don't expect a big selection no matter which broker you deal with. Although there may be dozens of choices out there in the bond universe, many of them will be unattainable through some brokers.

Worse, many discount brokers refuse to sell clients high-yield bonds, which are issued by companies with poor credit ratings and thus promise a higher return. Several of the big bank-owned discount brokers are in this group, and the motivation seems to be a desire to prevent clients from making bad investment decisions. It's odd, however, that a client can buy penny mining stocks without any nanny-like oversight, or buy on margin (i.e., with borrowed money) or buy cockamamie exchange-traded funds that invest in flaky stock indexes that no one follows. These types of investing activities are no riskier than buying high-yield bonds.

4. Playing Fair in the Selling of Mutual Funds

You may not realize it, but the fees charged by the vast majority of mutual funds includes a component that is earmarked to pay for investment advice. Take your typical big Canadian equity fund, with a management expense ratio of 2.25 per cent. Fully one percentage point of this amount goes not to the fund company, but to the adviser who sold the fund and his or her firm. In the industry, this fee is known as a trailing commission, or simply a trailer, and it's the way many advisers make their living.

Trailers are also the way discount brokers make some very decent coin. No, they don't provide advice—they *can't* advise you, in fact. And yet, they collect trailers just like advisers do. Some investors may not care about these unearned trailer fees because, overall, discount brokers are actually a pretty good place to buy funds. Most brokers have vast selections of funds for sale, and almost all are available with no purchase commissions or redemption fees. Still, there's something absurd about investors buying funds with MERs inflated by trailers that are collected by discount brokers that did little or nothing to earn them.

If you're perturbed by this, here are four steps you can take:

Buy no-load funds. No-load funds are offered by companies that sell direct to investors without any fees or commissions to buy or sell. Typically, they pay trailing commissions at about half the rate of conventional load funds, which means they have lower MERs. Good no-load fund families include Beutel Goodman, Mawer, McLean Budden and Phillips, Hager & North.

Buy Series D funds. RBC Direct Investing, Royal Bank of Canada's discount brokerage arm, sells this type of fund, which was specially created for DIY investors. Think of Series D funds as versions of all RBC's own funds with almost all the trailer stripped out. Here's an example: the RBC Canadian Dividend fund has a management expense ratio of 1.70 per cent, while the Series D version's MER is a svelte 1.15 per cent. You need to be an RBC Direct Investing client to buy Series D funds, and the minimum purchase is $10,000.

Consider dealing with Questrade. This small independent firm introduced a service in 2009 that rebates trailing commissions to clients in exchange for a monthly fee of $29.95. You need at least $36,000 in fund investments to make this worthwhile.

Buy exchange-traded funds. ETFs have ultra-low MERs that don't include trailers, and that makes them an ideal tool for do-it-yourself investors. Check out Chapter Three for more details on ETFs.

FIVE INVESTMENTS THAT GO GREAT IN DISCOUNT BROKERAGE ACCOUNTS

Discount brokerage accounts are kind of like the Costco of investing. You go in knowing what you want and are happy to forgo ambience and advice on what to buy because you know you're getting cheap prices. But as with those Costco retail stores, the choice at discount brokers is overwhelming. If it's available to Canadian investors, discount brokers sell it. Here are five investments that are definitely worth a look, and all are covered in more depth elsewhere in this book. They're recapped here simply to get you started as a DIY investor.

1. Exchange-Traded Funds

It's not only the low fees; ETFs are so versatile and easy to use that it takes only four or five to build a portfolio you can ride through the years with only some twiddling once twice a year to keep things in balance.

2. Blue-Chip Dividend Stocks

If you prefer to own individual stocks, dividend payers are your best bet. Most discount brokers offer dividend reinvestment plans (DRIPs) where your quarterly dividends are used to purchase more shares at little or no cost.

3. Global Stocks

There's no need to limit yourself to familiar Canadian names. All discount brokers offer access to major U.S. exchanges, where you'll find not only American companies listed, but also global companies that want to have their shares traded in the key U.S. market.

4. GICs from Alternative Banks, Small Trust Companies and Credit Unions

Better returns that you'll get from high-quality government bonds, and there's the benefit of deposit insurance for investments of up to $100,000 per bank or more from some credit unions.

5. Corporate Bonds

Yet another way to get higher returns than government bonds, although with somewhat higher levels of risk. The beauty of corporate bonds is that there's a wide spectrum of risk level and return. You can start with high-grade bank or insurance company bonds and go all the way down to high-yield bonds issued by more speculative businesses.

THREE COOL TOOLS OFFERED BY DISCOUNT BROKERAGES

Almost all discount brokerages offer a fairly similar level of research and financial planning tools for their clients. True fact: a lot of clients never use these tools, according to brokerage executives. It's a shame because many investors are making mistakes that just might have been prevented if they'd used resources that are freely available to them. Let's look at some of these resources.

1. Financial Planning and Asset Allocation Calculators

The financial crisis of 2008 taught investors the dangers of having too much of their portfolios in stocks. But how much is the right amount in terms of stocks, bonds and cash? One way to find out is to use the asset allocation calculators offered by almost all discount brokers these days.

These calculators aren't precision-guided weapons for mass investing success, so don't expect too much. But they are useful for translating your own personal investing goals and your risk tolerance into a reasonable mix of investments that will serve you well in both up and down markets. More simplistic calculators will focus on the matter of risk with a series of questions that probe your attitude toward losing money in the stock market. More sophisticated calculators will take a broader look at your personal situation by looking at your age, the amount of money you've already saved and the amount you're putting away currently.

When you're done answering questions, these calculators will often provide you with a portfolio blueprint that shows you how much of assets to put in all the various asset classes, including sub-categories like Canadian bonds and global bonds, and Canadian stocks, U.S. stocks and international stocks.

Asset allocation is a somewhat subjective discipline, a point that is emphatically shown in the way that recommended asset mixes vary among experts. So don't take what your discount broker's asset allocation calculator tells you as the one, true path to investing success. Rather, consider it as informed guidance that is well worth consulting.

2. Analyst Research on Stocks and Mutual Funds

Most discount brokers provide libraries of reports on stocks and, often, mutual funds that are written by professional analysts. Sometimes the analysts are employed by outside firms, and sometimes they're part of the same corporate family as the discount broker. Either way, these reports are a useful perk for the discount brokerage client.

We in the financial media pay a lot of attention to what brokerage analysts say about stocks. We sometimes report when these analysts upgrade or downgrade their ratings on a stock, and we often quote analysts when writing about a company they cover. The reason is simple: analysts are paid to study companies in depth and their views are worth considering.

Now, to the limitations of analyst research. One is the potential for bias. It's quite common for an analyst to cover a particular corporation that his or her firm is advising on a potential takeover or may be assisting with a stock issue. In other words, the company being rated is at the same time providing revenue to the brokerage firm. Following the collapse of the boom in technology stocks in 2001–02, there was intense focus on the role of analysts in helping to pump up stocks that didn't merit the hype. Brokerage firms have taken steps to make the work of their analysts more transparent and accountable, but the wise investor understands that there is still the potential for bias.

So how do you effectively use an analyst report? By treating it as a second opinion on a stock or mutual fund you've already been thinking about, or as a starting point for doing more research. Don't buy anything just because an analyst rates it a "buy" or "strong buy," and don't automatically dump anything that is downgraded to "underperform" or something like that. Investigate why the analyst has developed that opinion and then assess how valid the view is with further research.

3. Guided Portfolios

I get why these aren't more popular with do-it-yourself investors. DIY types are often mavericks who see themselves as having rejected the investing establishment in favour of making their own decisions. I applaud this sentiment, but with a proviso. To be a true maverick investor, you need some serious financial chops.

Guided portfolios are what you use when you don't have the time or knowledge to choose your own portfolio. They're groupings of mutual funds or exchange-traded funds that are tailored to your particular profile as an investor—high-, medium- or low-risk tolerance, and an emphasis on growth or income. You could easily find individual portfolio building blocks yourself, but guided portfolios do the work for you.

Don't be a sucker, though. Recognize that guided portfolios are, on occasion, nothing more than a tool to load you up with in-house mutual funds and thus generate lots of fee revenue for your broker and the bank that owns it. The problem with these portfolios is that they virtually always have a weak link. A fund family may be great at Canadian equity funds and bond funds, but useless at U.S. and global investing. That's why I always prefer guided portfolios using funds from a variety of families. I just trust them more.

Investment advisers sell a lot of guided portfolios, which are also called wrap accounts. So what's the benefit of a guided portfolio from a discount broker? Simple—lower costs. Your broker's guided portfolio should be made up of low-fee funds that give you the opportunity to reap higher returns. It's for this reason that guided portfolios made up of ultra-cheap ETFs are so appealing (see Chapter Three for the lowdown on ETFs).

**THREE ONLINE RESOURCES THAT DIY INVESTORS SHOULD
CERTAINLY USE**

Investing for yourself means doing lots of research (or it should).
Whether you're trawling for investing ideas or looking for a second
opinion on stocks or funds you've found on your own, you're going to
need some resources you can count on for straight-up, unbiased
information. Here are some of my favourites.

1. Morningstar Canada (morningstar.ca)

In the United States, Morningstar has built a respected role as
a provider of unbiased reports on mutual funds, exchange-
traded funds and stocks. Because it's strictly an analysis firm
and not a seller of investments or adviser to corporations,
Morningstar can say anything it wants in its commentary. That
same unvarnished analysis is what you get from Morningstar
Canada, which covers funds and ETFs sold here.

Morningstar has a five-star rating system for funds, but that's
just trivia for simpletons who think it's possible to tell what a
fund will do in the future by looking at a rating of its past performance (news bulletin: past returns are a feeble indicator of
future results). The best resource on the Morningstar website
is its list of Fund Analyst Picks, which are mutual funds that
have been selected by in-house analysts as the best of the best.

This is no popularity contest. The last time I looked at the
list of favourites, one of the names was Brandes Global Equity,
which was a barking dog of a fund at the time with a twelve-
month loss of 35.5 per cent and a five-year compound average
annual loss of 3.8 per cent. Morningstar's people liked the fund

because of strong management with excellent long-term results and a contrarian bent for taking positions in undervalued stocks it likes, no matter what the overall market is doing. Were the Morningstar analysts right on Brandes Global Equity? Go to Morningstar.ca and find out. While you're there, look up any funds you've been eyeing and read any available analyst reports on them. What they provide is Grade A material for do-it-yourself investors looking for a second opinion.

2. Dominion Bond Rating Service (dbrs.com)

Bond rating agencies lost some respect in the early stages of the big financial crisis by not highlighting the dangers of mortgage-based securities that they had rated. As we now know, mortgage loans made to Americans who couldn't really afford them were bundled into securities that were snapped up by financial firms of all types around the world. As mortgage defaults mounted, these mortgage-based securities plunged in value and undermined the financial health of everyone that owned them. This is a bit of a digression, but it's worth pursuing because it points to the fallibility of bond raters. They just didn't probe hard enough in this case.

Now, for the case in favour of bond raters. Whereas stock analysts at investment houses ultimately focus on whether a company's stock will go up or down, bond raters delve into a company's financial well-being. After all, the whole point of rating bonds is to discern how able a company is to meet its obligations to pay interest on its bonds and redeem them at maturity. The worst thing that can happen when you own a bond is for the issuing company to default. Bond raters are supposed to warn you about the risks of this happening.

Obviously, then, bond raters are worth consulting if you're looking at a corporate or government bond and want to know how safe it is. But they can also have worthwhile things to say if you're looking at buying a company's shares and wondering about the underlying financials. DBRS is a major bond rater here in Canada and it makes its ratings and news releases available at no charge on its websites (you have to be a subscriber to get the full rating report).

3. Show Me the Return (showmethereturn.com)

This website is maintained by Second Opinion Investor Services, a growing financial-advice firm that does exactly what its name suggests. For a flat fee, an adviser will go over your current investment plan and see if it's on track. The Second Opinion people built the Show Me the Return website as a kind of self-promotional exercise, but it's one that benefits investors, too, because it offers a way for them to gauge how well their portfolios are performing.

The correct way to measure investment returns is to compare them to the correct mix of benchmarks. Your Canadian equity funds or stocks should be compared to the S&P/TSX composite index, or maybe the S&P/TSX 60 index if you only hold big blue-chip stocks. Your bonds should be compared to the DEX Universe Bond Index (you may know this index better under its old Scotia name), your blue-chip U.S. holdings should be compared to the S&P 500 stock index and your holdings outside North America to the MSCI Europe Australasia Far East (EAFE) Index.

Benchmarking is a somewhat complicated exercise unless you have quick and easy access to the right data. Show Me the Return gives you this access. You simply fill in the percentages of your portfolio in each of the major asset classes and then let the website tell you what the blended benchmark return is. That's what you compare your portfolio against.

Show Me the Return will also help you calculate your portfolio's annualized rate of return, a piece of information that is glaringly absent from the account statements issued by many financial firms. It's a somewhat laborious process to input all the necessary information, but it's worth the effort to find out how your investments are performing.

SIX

INVESTMENT ADVISERS

THE ULTIMATE INSULT ONE ADVISER can hurl at another is to call him or her a mutual fund salesperson. I love this because it vividly conveys the fact that advisers are supposed to do more than sell investments. Actually, what the good advisers sell is advice. To these pros, investments are simply the medium through which most financial goals are reached. This chapter is devoted to helping you find a true adviser and avoid mutual fund salespeople. Warning: Finding a good adviser is harder work than you imagine.

TEN TRAITS OF A GREAT ADVISER

Yes, huge investment returns are evidence of good financial advice. But if that's the only thing your adviser has going for him or her, then you're headed for trouble. The reason is that no one who manages money for a living can sustain superb results indefinitely. When the hard times come, strong advisers are able to keep their client relationships healthy thanks to the multifaceted quality service they've provided over the years. Here are some traits of good advisers that I've observed over the years.

1. Knows His or Her Client

KYC, or know your client, is a basic concept in providing financial advice. It's all about ensuring that clients are only put in suitable investments that agree with their investing objectives. Advisers are required to familiarize themselves with their clients at the outset and fill out certain forms that set out the client's particulars. How this process is completed separates the good advisers from the rest.

There are a number of ways to get at a person's risk tolerance, and one of the most common is to use a questionnaire that asks questions like "How would you feel if your portfolio averaged 10 per cent annually but lost 40 per cent in a year?" Savvy advisers know that a client might easily say he'd be fine with this scenario, but melt with anxiety when that 40-per-cent decline comes. That's why these advisers go into more depth when probing a client's investing profile.

It's all about asking detailed questions about you and your financial background so as to gather the information needed to assess how conservative, balanced or aggressive your portfolio should be. You say you want to go for the gusto, stock market downturns be damned? Good advisers never take that at face value.

2. Provides More than Investment Advice

The main reason why many people have an adviser is to help them invest to realize goals like a university education for their kids or a comfortable retirement. Investments are how you build the wealth necessary to reaching these goals, so they'll be a big part of what you and your adviser talk about. But investments are merely tools, not an end in themselves.

To properly put investments to work, you need a financial plan that looks at where you are and where you want to go, and then maps out a route. The best advisers find out how much money you need to reach your goals and what kind of a rate a return you'll require. Only then does the search for investments begin.

The most useful advisers do even more for you. Some can help you get the best deal on a mortgage, ensure you're properly insured, minimize your income tax bill and ensure a smooth transition of your wealth to your kids or whomever else you designate.

3. Keeps in Touch with You

You'll see a lot of your adviser when you first sign on as a client. There are forms to fill out, your financial history and aspirations to discuss and investments to consider. The amount of contact you have with your adviser from there on tells the story of whether you're valued as a client.

Face-to-face meetings at least once per year are pretty much mandatory. Periodic phone calls, especially amid rough days for the stock markets, are basic. Don't view this contact as simple client-stroking, because it's more than that. You can't responsibly dispense investment advice and then walk away from a client. Stuff happens in people's lives, and the financial markets are always in flux. That's why good advisers stay in touch.

4. Makes It Clear How He or She Is Paid, and Is Comfortable in Doing So

There are three ways advisers can be paid—through fees and commissions related to the sale of investments, through a fee of 1 to 2 per cent of your assets per year, or through a flat fee or hourly rate. Which is best? The simple answer is that the best method is whichever one is used by an adviser who is a good fit for you. In other words, find the right person, *then* deal with how he or she is compensated.

One way you'll know you've got a good adviser is if he explains, without you having to demand it, how he is paid. In the companion volume to this book, *How to Pay Less and Save More for Yourself: The Essential Canadian Consumer Guide to Banking and Investing,* I go into great detail on adviser compensation and how to discuss it intelligently with your own chosen financial professional. Here, suffice it to say that you want an adviser who is not only forthright about compensation, but is also relaxed about it.

Advisers like this have no problem discussing fees because they're trained professionals who require and deserve adequate compensation for their work. A dodgy attitude toward fees is a sign of an adviser who lacks integrity—probably, a mutual fund salesperson.

5. Keeps a Close Eye on the Fees You Pay to Own Investments

For almost every retail investment product you can name, there's some basic math that determines your ultimate return. Here it is: gross return minus fees equals net returns that are reported to investors. The lesson here is that fees eat into returns. Minimize fees and there's more left over to put into your pocket.

Given this basic reality of investing, it should kind of disgust you to learn that there are a significant number of advisers who dismiss fees as an issue when selecting products for their clients. I may be overly cynical in saying this, but my concern about advisers of this ilk is that they're selling expensive products larded with fees that reward them and leave less for clients. Advisers who put clients first naturally pay attention to the fees their clients must pay.

Fees are far from the sole consideration when selecting investments, so don't expect a good adviser to automatically sell you the lowest-fee products in any particular category.

How can you test your adviser on fees? Ask this question when presented with a recommendation to buy a new mutual fund or other product: What are the fees, and how do they compare to similar products? The good adviser will tell you the cost in plain terms, and then cheerfully explain how the fees meshed with the many other considerations that went into selecting this investment.

6. Has Told You to Sell Some of Your Best-Performing Investments and Buy More of Your Worst Performers

This is a sign of a real pro. Think about it: you have to call up a client and tell her to sell some of her best investments—her home runs—and use the money to buy more of the stuff that just ain't working in her portfolio. This is contrary to human nature, which is to buy more of what works and ignore, or even sell, what it isn't.

The impressive part about an adviser telling clients to make these changes is not the fact that he or she is practising something called rebalancing (that's where you find an appropriate mix of assets and then adjust your holdings once or twice a year to ensure you stay within that mix). No, the truly notable aspect of this approach is how it displays the faith an adviser has in his or her approach and choice of investments. If an adviser has this much confidence, it's a positive sign they've done some homework.

7. Admits Mistakes

Adviser mistakes, almost by definition, cost you money. But it's possible to divide these mistakes into two levels of severity: those that are ruinously bad and require you to seek compensation, and those that are more routine and ultimately forgivable. Before deciding between the two sides, you should know that investing is one of those areas of human endeavour where success is measured by being right more often than you're wrong.

Yes, mistakes will be made, whether you have an adviser to guide your investing or you make your own decisions. Good advisers mitigate any harm from the bad decisions they make with their good, sound calls. They also admit their mistakes.

This is not a matter of calling you up and offering a grovelling mea culpa. Rather, it's simply admitting when a decision goes wrong and explaining the broader context—revisiting why the decision was made in the first place, how it went wrong and what will be done to fix things. Advisers will inevitably make mistakes; how they're handled is what distinguishes good advisers from bad.

8. Makes You Feel Like a Valued Customer, No Matter How Large Your Portfolio

We must face the reality that advisers make more money from clients with big accounts than they do from small clients. If your portfolio is valued at less than, say, $100,000, you can forget about any expectations you might have of regular personal contact with your adviser.

With a large account in seven figures or the high sixes, you should expect to have a direct pipeline to your adviser. Don't settle for being shunted off to an assistant or associate, unless you're only raising a minor point. People with large accounts should also pay the lowest fees, and receive the fullest possible range of services.

A good adviser tells clients with small accounts exactly what they can expect. Example: "If I'm not available to answer one of your questions right away, you'll be referred to my associate so as to avoid any delays in getting you the information you need. My associate's name is so-and-so, and here are the qualifications that convinced me to put her on my team." There's no doubt, though, that an adviser cannot make a client feel welcome without personalized periodic personal contact, whether over the phone or in person.

9. Brings Risk into the Conversation When Discussing Investment Products

There are two elements to consider in every investment decision: risk and reward. Rewards we all know about—they're why we invest in stocks and equity funds, commodities, real estate and other stuff that can soar in value. Some investors put risk first, and the number is undoubtedly higher after what happened in 2008. Still, it's worth hammering home the point that an investment product's potential rewards should never be looked at without considering the related risks.

This is where a good adviser comes in. She quells enthusiasm for high-flying stock markets by talking about those inevitable downturns, and she does the opposite as well. Yes, it's possible to take too little risk in a portfolio (the danger is that you won't generate high enough investment returns to meet your goals), and it's an adviser's job to point this out, too.

10. Stands Up to You When You're Wrong

"No, I will not buy you some Nortel Networks shares trading at $120."

"No, I won't sell all your low-yielding dividend stocks and bonds and build you a portfolio of only income trusts."

"No, I don't think it's a good idea to base your portfolio on bank stocks."

These imaginary adviser comments summarize the ways in which investors have had to be protected from themselves over the past decade. The first example comes from the technology boom that saw Nortel Networks shares top out at about $120 in 2000 before a long slide to worthlessness. The second is from the income trust boom that fizzled when the federal government decided trusts were gaining too much influence in the marketplace and announced new tax on them for 2011. The third example was from 2007, when banks appeared to be bargain-priced but in fact were on the verge of much worse declines in 2008 and 2009.

If you have an adviser, it's likely because you've understood you don't have enough investing knowledge to look after your own money. A good adviser will recognize this and stand up to you when your lack of knowledge leads you to suggest doing something stupid.

TEN SIGNS OF A ROTTEN ADVISER

Let's face it—you probably know in your gut that you've got a useless investment adviser. But let's take a look at some true signs of bad adviser behaviour that should get you thinking about making a switch.

1. You never hear from your adviser.

What this tells you is that your adviser sees you as a being like an orange—squeeze out the juice and discard. This sort of adviser is all about building wealth—for him. He gets you to buy into a portfolio of recommended mutual funds or a hotshot wrap account and collects his reward in the form of various fees and commissions. You, the client, are immaterial once you've handed over your money. By the way, adviser newsletters or emailed form letters do not qualify as contact. Mainly, they're junk mail.

2. You never heard from your adviser during the market crash of 2008.

I remember speaking to advisers who spent most of their time in the fall of 2008 trying to calm panicky clients and explain that the world as we know it was not ending. One particular adviser made it a point to call several clients a day and then spend as long as was needed on the phone with them to answer questions and provide comforting commentary on how the markets always rebounded from past meltdowns. If your adviser never called you as the markets floundered, there are two explanations: he placed no value on you as a client, or he was too embarrassed and/or cowardly to face up to what had become of your investments.

3. You have no written financial plan.

This is a touchy one because there are advisers out there who provide good, solid investment guidance and not much more. Maybe that's enough for their clients. It shouldn't be, though. True professional advisers understand that a written financial plan is like a blueprint for helping clients articulate and then reach their goals. Without a plan, the adviser-client relationship may come down to nothing more than talking about how your investments are doing. Don't be put off if an adviser tells you you'll have to pay a fee for the plan. This may be a signal that the adviser is planning to put some real work into the plan and wants fair compensation.

4. Your whole relationship with your adviser is based on the sale of investments.

If all you want as an investor is to have some guidance in setting up a portfolio, then your basic fund salesperson may suffice. But don't mistake this kind of service for what you get with a proper adviser. Investment advice is part of the deal, of course, but retirement and tax planning should be included, plus maybe estate planning, guidance on managing debt and even some input on your insurance needs. Advisers will typically provide different mixes of these types of services, but the common theme is that they do more than sell mutual funds.

5. You're always being urged to make changes in your investments. The typical investor is best served with a diversified, well-constructed portfolio that takes all eventualities into consideration and thus needs only minor tending on an ongoing basis. If your adviser wants you to be more active as a client, you have to ask why. Is it because she believes that active trading is a better way to make money? In fact, it almost never is. Is it because she's trying to generate fees and commissions generated through active trading? This is a huge concern because it's a clear sign that your adviser is putting her interests ahead of yours. If you suspect your adviser of generating wasteful trading in your account, gather up all your recent transactions and ask for an accounting of how well they've worked out for you. Extreme cases of excessive trading are called churning. Go right to your adviser's boss if you see this happening.

6. You hear constant hype about new investing products you should buy.
Here's a rule of investing they don't talk about very much: no matter how smartly thought out a new investing product sounds, you can never go wrong by taking a pass on it. I simply cannot remember the last new investing product that I thought people really should buy. Was it principal-protected notes? No way. Life-cycle funds (the asset mix changes as you get older and more risk-averse)? No again. Structured products (they used all

kinds of black-box manoeuvres to wring a juicy flow of income from a portfolio of stocks)? No, no, a thousand times no. I concede that there may be a new product in the future that will have wide applicability to investors, and I also concede that some advisers may be able to make a case for some new products in specific instances. But an adviser who keeps pushing new products is simply looking for commission income.

7. You feel your adviser is pushing the envelope in terms of risk.
Have some empathy for the position the adviser is in. Some clients say they want to invest conservatively and then grumble when their returns are commensurately low. Also, some clients will chafe if a killjoy adviser tries to block them from making a late jump onto the most recent investing bandwagon. This is all background to help you understand why advisers will sometimes bump up the risk level of a client's portfolio. Ideally, higher risk means higher returns, and that means happy clients who don't complain about missing all the fun going on in the stock market. Here's the problem with that approach: it inevitably—and this word is used after some consideration—leads to an unnecessarily large loss in a client's portfolio during a bear market. The best advisers will err on the safe side with clients, not push the risk level higher.

8. You have no clue how your portfolio is doing.
Let's get interactive for a moment. Put this book down and go grab a copy of an account statement for your RRSP, RESP, RRIF, TFSA or regular investment account. Scan the pages to see whether you can find out the most important piece of

information there is in investing: your rate of return. Can't find the magic number? Amazingly, there are many financial firms out there that don't provide this information. They tell you what your account was worth last month or quarter and what it's worth now, but not your annualized returns or how much you've made or lost since you set up the account. If your account statements aren't showing you the right data about returns, then your adviser should be doing the job. Investing without knowing how much you're making or losing is just stupid. It's like driving without knowing where you're going.

9. It's jargon city when you talk to your adviser.
The clearest sign of expertise in a particular profession or subject area is the ability to explain technical terms in language that a complete layman can easily understand. If you're an experienced investor and your adviser talks to you in jargon, that's fine. But if you're a layman and you're getting bombarded with baffling technical terms by your adviser, you have to wonder what's going on. It may be that your adviser simply needs to be reminded to keep things clear. Or it may be you've got a fund salesperson who knows how to talk the talk of the investing big boys, but not actually explain it to regular clients. Here are some examples of how jargon can be replaced by everyday language: the term *fees* can be used instead of MERs (management expense ratios); the words *stocks and bonds* or *guaranteed investment certificates* can be substituted for *equities* and *fixed income*; the term *volatility* can be avoided and instead the adviser can talk about the risk of losing money.

10. You have too many investments in your portfolio.

Investment advisers often get new clients who have left another adviser for various reasons. I've heard advisers I respect tell me that one sure sign a new client has been dealing in the past with an amateur is a portfolio overloaded with different mutual funds. I've heard of cases where investors might hold several dozen or more different funds, which is extreme overkill.

There are no widely recognized rules for how many funds investors should have in their portfolios. Really, it's a matter of diversification and portfolio size. You want exposure to a wide variety of categories, but you don't need exposure to everything. Getting the impression your adviser is trying to cover off everything in your portfolio? That's a sign of guesswork and trend-chasing.

FIVE KILLER INTERVIEW QUESTIONS THAT WILL HELP YOU AVOID HIRING A DEADHEAD ADVISER

Finding the right investment adviser is a process that is not unlike hiring a new employee to fill an important job posting. You need to find a candidate who not only has the right background and technical expertise, but who is a good fit emotionally. Here are some questions to ask a prospective adviser that go beyond such basic subjects as his or her credentials and work experience and the way in which he or she is paid.

1. What will you do for me besides sell me investments?

If a lot of advisers were to answer this question honestly, they'd reply by saying "nothing." That's because they're essentially sellers of investment products and nothing more. A quality adviser provides much more, including varying degrees of tax and estate planning and advice on managing debt. All this advice will flow from an overarching financial plan that maps out what you need to do to reach your financial goals. If it's all about the investments when talking to an adviser, then keep looking.

2. Can I speak to a couple of your clients?
Providing references is a basic way of establishing credibility. A good adviser with happy clients should have the foresight to ask a few of them to be on call to provide a reference should a prospective new customer request one. Ask references how their accounts have done, what kind of advice they're receiving that isn't investment-related and how often they hear from their adviser. Just for fun, ask as well about how their adviser handled the market meltdown that began in 2008. If you get any static at all from an adviser when requesting a reference, then keep looking.

3. What's your view on the importance of costs in choosing investments?
One sure way to smoke out an adviser who's only concerned with selling stuff is to raise this question. Serious, thoughtful advisers know that the cost of owning an investment has a direct bearing on how attractive it is to own. It's not the only factor, but it's one of the more important ones. If you hear an adviser scoffing at costs—and, most likely, telling you that performance is what matters—then keep looking.

4. What's your view on indexing?

This question flows out of the previous one. Advisers who are highly sensitive to the costs their clients pay tend to believe in indexing, which means buying low-cost products that mimic the returns of stock and bond indexes. Indexing is the opposite of active management, which is what higher-cost mutual funds do in choosing stocks and bonds for clients. I'm a believer in indexing, but many reputable advisers prefer active management (whether with funds or picking their own stocks). That's fine. If an adviser isn't an indexing adherent, then he or she should at least recognize the value of this investing approach. The test is whether an adviser trashes indexing, and many will. If this happens, then keep looking.

5. How much time will you be able to give me, based on my account size?

The preferred answer here is an honest one, not one the adviser thinks is going to make you happy. So if you have a small or middling account, you should be given a frank assessment of how much face time you and your adviser will spend together. Seek specifics—will you be dealing with the adviser himself or his lackeys? Will you speak by phone periodically and have an annual face-to-face meeting or will it all be done by email? If you have a substantial account—let's arbitrarily say something solidly in the six-figure range, at least—then you should expect a higher level of contact. If an adviser isn't professional enough to tell you what level of service you can expect, then keep looking.

THREE REASONS TO BE SKEPTICAL OF FEE-BASED ACCOUNTS

Several years ago, fee-based accounts were considered to be the future as far as financial advice was concerned. Clients would pay their adviser a fee set as a percentage of their account assets (usually 1 to 2 per cent), thereby eliminating the conflicts of interest that are ever-present when an adviser makes a living off of commissions. No more would clients have to worry that an adviser was recommending a particular product because it paid the most lucrative fees, nor would they have to be concerned that the trades an adviser was recommending were strictly meant to generate fee revenue. Fee-based accounts have become reasonably popular in recent years, but they're far from a slam-dunk choice for all investors. Here are three reasons to be wary of these accounts.

1. You're paying for service, whether you receive it or not.
If you have an effective, hard-working adviser, the fee-based model makes good sense. But what if you're paying a steady flow of fees to an adviser who has done little for you other than come up with a list of mutual funds to buy? This is the nightmare scenario of the fee-based account.

Arguably, advisers in a fee-based account should work harder than their commission-based counterparts. The fees paid by the client are out in the open, and so should the service provided by the adviser. To me, the fee-based adviser isn't earning his or her keep unless clients are getting not only investment advice, but also basic financial planning that covers retirement saving, tax and debt strategies, estate planning and possibly insurance.

Before you sign up for a fee-based account, ask for an exact accounting of what you, the client, get in exchange for your fees. A top adviser will have a ready answer, whereas a dead-head will be stuck for an answer.

2. You're paying for trades, whether or not you're a frequent trader.
A classic sign of a predatory adviser is one who is constantly bugging you to make changes in your portfolio. Most of the time, the adviser's goal here is to generate commission and fee income. Fee-based accounts do away with this issue by including trading costs in the account fee clients pay. But here's a thought: what if you're a buy-and-hold investor who has a nice portfolio of bonds and blue-chip stocks and who doesn't want or need to trade much?

The practice of advisers putting buy-and-hold investors, particularly seniors, in fee-based accounts has been a particular problem in the United States. A few years ago, a major investment dealer paid $23.3 million (U.S.) to settle an action launched by the New York State Attorney General's office over clients who were steered into fee-based accounts. In one case, a ninety-one-year-old who made four trades over two years paid fees of $35,000.

3. You have a conservative portfolio mainly built with bonds or GICs.
Again, seniors are the most at risk here. Imagine a seventy-five-year-old with three-quarters of her portfolio in bonds or GICs and the rest in stocks or mutual funds. With bond yields as low as they've been this decade, it simply doesn't make good financial sense for her to pay an account fee of 1 to 2 per cent.

Some investment firms will charge a lower level of fees on the bond portion of a client's portfolio, and that may help make a fee-based account more palatable. Still, you've got to seriously question the value of a fee-based account if you're a conservative investor who mainly wants GICs and bonds. How hard is it to buy these on your own?

SEVEN STEPS TO TAKE IF YOUR ADVISER HAS MADE YOU POORER

Let's be clear about something: you can have a very fine investment adviser and still lose money. In a year like 2008, when the stock markets were down in the neighbourhood of 40 per cent from their peaks, success is measured in degrees of loss. If you lost less than the market (stocks and bonds), then you've done comparatively well. If you lost more, particularly over a long period of time, then your adviser has some explaining to do. Don't like the answers you get? Then here are the steps to take.

1. Contact the branch manager in your adviser's office.
The branch manager's job is to supervise all the advisers in a particular location. So in a sense, this is your adviser's boss. Lay out your complaint with as much detail as possible when contacting a branch manager, and make it clear what you're looking for in terms of compensation. Don't expect much from the branch manager, especially if your account is on the smaller side.

2. Contact the compliance department for the firm where your adviser works.
An investment firm's compliance department has the job of

making sure all securities regulations are being followed and to address situations where this is not happening. If your adviser has been doing something egregious—churning your account to generate trading commissions, for example—then compliance should have caught this.

3. If you deal with a bank-owned firm, go to the bank's own ombudsman.

All the big banks have ombudsman's offices to address complaints from clients that have not been handled by front-line staff. These ombudsman's offices look into complaints about all aspects of a bank's relationship with clients, including investing matters.

4. Go to the Ombudsman for Banking Services and Investments (OBSI).

OBSI is a free service with its own investigators that can recommend that a firm make restitution of up to $350,000. OBSI is an option for people who deal with investment firms that don't have their own ombudsmen, and for those who have struck out trying to get a bank ombudsman to address their concerns. You can reach OBSI at 1-888-451-4519, or 416-287-2877 in the Toronto area. The web address is obsi.ca.

5. Hire a lawyer.

This can be a costly process if you end up in a protracted legal proceeding, but a lawyer experienced in representing investors can sometimes get a settlement offer in fairly short order. Some lawyers will represent investors on a fee-for-service basis and some will work on a contingency basis, where they take a percentage of any award you receive. It's generally thought that your losses must be in excess of $100,000 to make it economical to hire a lawyer.

6. Seek arbitration.

The Investment Industry Regulatory Organization of Canada (IIROC) offers an arbitration program to resolve disputes between investors and member investment firms. If an investor requests arbitration, an IIROC member must agree to participate. There are fees to use the service—hiring a lawyer to make your case would add to the cost—and the maximum an investor can be awarded is $100,000 plus interest and arbitration costs. You can reach IIROC at 416-364-6133, or iiroc.ca.

7. Complain to IIROC or the Mutual Fund Dealers Association of Canada.

These industry organizations can't order a firm to make good your losses, but they can discipline advisers and firms that have broken securities regulations. If you think your adviser is a serial offender or has done something unethical or illegal, you'd be doing your fellow investors a favour by alerting IIROC or the MFDA. The IIROC's toll-free complaints line can be reached at 1-877-442-4322, and the web address is iiroc.ca. The MFDA's complaint line is at 1-888-466-6332, and the web address is mfda.ca.

SEVEN

INFORMATION, PLEASE

INVESTING IS AN EVER-CHANGING DISCIPLINE in which
the unknowledgeable and complacent are certain to be vic-
timized. Mistakes aren't just learning experiences—they can
also be costly disasters that undermine your efforts to save for
retirement or send your kids to university. Think you know
enough to qualify as a savvy investor? New products and services are being introduced all the time, and they demand
careful study in almost every case. Also, the conventional
thinking about matters like building portfolios and managing risk is constantly evolving. For these reasons, investors of
all types need resources to build their understanding of the
markets and financial products. This section of the book
highlights some places that will help investors at all levels of
knowledge make smarter, more profitable decisions.

FIVE PLACES BEGINNERS SHOULD GO TO GET SMARTER ABOUT INVESTING

Beginners have special requirements in terms of the resources they need to learn about investing. Clarity is key, and that means jargon has to be kept to a minimum. Effective learning material for beginners also has to be free of the sales hype that can subtly contaminate the helpful educational brochures and websites offered by the financial industry.

1. The Investor Education Fund Website (investored.ca)

The IEF is an offshoot of the Ontario Securities Commission, and it is funded through penalties levied against those who break securities regulations in the province. Not a penny of support comes from the investment industry, which means the information presented on the fund's voluminous website is free of any bias, tilt, spin or anything else designed to move readers toward one product versus another.

The fund has taken great care to ensure the material it presents is both accurate and comprehensible for investing rookies. Contributing writers all have recognized financial credentials, and efforts have clearly been made to ensure that no one will walk away from this website complaining it's too hard to understand.

There are two ways to use the IEF website. You can treat it like an investing encyclopedia, where you jump in strategically to learn about specific issues of interest like how mutual fund fees work or what kind of returns it's reasonable to expect from the stock market. Or you can use the site as a sort of online investing how-to book. To get started, just look under the heading Money and Investing and click on Investing Basics. From there, you can work your way through various "chapters"—much of the material is actually presented in point form—that touch on things like risk and the correct mix of investments.

A question I've probably been asked about ten thousand times in my years as personal-finance columnist at *The Globe and Mail* is how to find a good financial adviser. One of the IEF website's most popular features is titled "Advisers: Who should you trust with your money?" It's one of the better primers around on the subject. Other highlights on the site include a collection of online tools and calculators. The next time some know-nothing starts blathering about how fees don't matter when investing in mutual funds, direct them to the mutual fund fee calculator on this website.

QuickSurvey: Ten of the Most-Viewed Resources on the Investor Education Fund Website

1) How do I start saving for retirement?
2) Risk comfort level quiz
3) RRSP savings calculator
4) How do I balance retirement savings with other goals?
5) Poor adviser practices that can be harmful to your financial health
6) How your adviser is paid
7) What questions should I ask before I choose an adviser?
8) Mutual fund fee impact calculator
9) TFSA vs. RRSP: which one is right for you?
10) What is a GIC?

2. Investopedia (investopedia.com)

This website is, as the name suggests, an online investing encyclopedia. It's the kind of website you bookmark and then revisit as necessary to look up terms you don't understand or on which you need more information. Investopedia is part of the Forbes financial media empire, but it was founded back in 1999 by a couple of guys from Edmonton, Cory Janssen and Cory Wagner, and it has lots of Canadian content.

Let's say you're new to investing in stocks and you keep coming across mentions of the price–earnings ratio, or P/E. Type this term into Investopedia's search box and you'll find a simple and brief explanation of how the P/E is a company's share price divided by its earnings per share, or EPS. If that's not enough detail for you, there are links to longer articles with lots more information. One such article explains the important lesson that the P/E ratio is much more revealing than share price in determining how pricey a stock is. A $10 stock with a P/E of 75, it explains, is much more expensive than a $100 stock with a P/E of 20. Another article highlights an alternative measure of how expensive a stock is, the PEG ratio—the P/E ratio divided by annual growth in earnings per share.

Investopedia also features a variety of articles listed by topic, like bonds, investing basics, exchange-traded funds (ETFs) and options and futures. The Investing Basics area offers useful information under headings like "Seven Forehead-Slapping Stock Blunders," "Do You Need a Financial Advisor?" and "In Praise of Portfolio Simplicity."

The material on the site is written by experts, many of whom are financial professionals. Their bylines and biographies appear, and you can email the writers with comments and questions.

3. Independent Investor (independentinvestor.info)

The appeal of this website is that its creator, Marc Ryan, is an ex-securities regulator and money manager. So he knows how the financial industry works, both for and against individual investors like you. Ryan makes it clear from the start that if you read the material on his website, you're getting unbiased information from a source that has no ties to banks, brokers or insurers.

This website works along similar lines to the one operated by the Investor Education Fund. It's less slick, but still cleverly designed. Pick a topic and you'll find a series of chapters to browse through, each liberally sprinkled with links to other websites that provide additional information. There are also lots of pop-up boxes to help explain things.

Another reason to visit this site regularly is that Ryan posts a steady stream of new articles on the home page that cover both topical and non-topical investing issues. When I visited the site while writing this book, there was a smart analysis of preferred shares that addressed the question of whether this type of security is too volatile for conservative investors seeking income. Ryan leans toward the view that they are too prone to bouncing around in price, although he thought that the availability of preferred-share exchange-traded funds might mitigate this problem by allowing investors to cheaply buy a diversified basket of preferred shares. As usual, this article was full of links to useful nuggets of information, including articles by journalists and ETF websites.

As is so often the case with investor advocates, Ryan is a big proponent of index investing and ETFs (Chapter Three has the lowdown on ETFs) and a critic of mutual funds. Even if you disagree, you'll find his arguments against funds to be thought-provoking. Oh, and be sure to sign up for the weekly newsletter he sends out to keep readers abreast of new material being added.

4. Financial Webring (financialwebring.org)

This website is partly a valuable directory of other websites and blogs that cover a wide range of investing topics, and partly a well-used online forum where members can pose and answer questions from fellow investors.

If you're an investing beginner, go to the forum and check out the section called Starting Out on the Right Track. You'll find topics here ranging from whether it's best to use an adviser or a discount broker to where GIC rates are heading to how to measure the performance of a portfolio.

Got a specific topic you want to know more about—like, say, dividend investing (a fine topic if ever there was one)? You could jump into the Stock Picking area of the forum and start reading threads like "The Power of Dividend Growth." Or you could use the search engine to comb through the site for mentions of, say, bank stocks or dividend-focused exchange-traded funds.

The people participating in the forums are well informed and they love a good argument, which means you'll often find a fierce debate going. That said, newcomers shouldn't be afraid to ask basic questions. You'd be surprised how your fellow investors can sometimes explain things that investing professionals can't talk about without resorting to jargon-filled mumblings. Note: There is a new alternative to Financial Webring called Canadian Money Forum at canadianmoneyforum.com

5. Bylo Selhi (bylo.org)

Bylo Selhi is the punning moniker of a public-spirited Canadian who has created a website to educate do-it-yourself investors. This site, which is part of the Financial Webring community, bills itself as being about "smart mutual fund investing for independent investors." But there's a clear editorial bias toward indexing and the use of exchange-traded funds rather than mutual funds.

Interested in learning more about ETFs? Bylo Selhi has a special section devoted to the topic, and it's stuffed with links to other sites where you can do many days' worth of research. Prefer widely available index funds to ETFs, which can only be bought if you have a brokerage account? Bylo's got that topic covered as well. He also can be counted on to present articles from various publications that make the argument for index investing. Rounding out the package is a directory of links to dozens of websites of interest to investors.

SEVEN GREAT INVESTING WEBSITES TO BOOKMARK

I clearly recall what a revelation it was back at the beginning of this decade when investing websites began to proliferate. Before the Internet, you had to wait until tomorrow's newspaper to find out how your stocks did. If a stock made news, you had to wait until the next day as well to get all the details. As for charting stocks, viewing corporate financial data and finding out what analysts were saying, that was beyond your reach unless you had a stockbroker to feed you the information. Today, investing websites make all this info available at no cost. The only complication: there are dozens of sites to choose from, some of them superb and others just mediocre or worse. I use investing websites all the time in my work, and here are the ones I've found to be the most useful for everyday investors. Note: You can add the educational websites mentioned earlier to the list below.

1. Globeinvestor (globeinvestor.com)

The Globe and Mail—the newspaper I work for—put a lot of effort into a relaunch of Globeinvestor in spring 2009, enhancing this website's status as the top online destination for Canadian investors. The other sites on this list all have their uses, and I encourage you to explore them. But if you're primarily interested in Canadian stocks, no U.S.–owned site compares to Globeinvestor in terms of its blend of market data on stocks listed on the TSX, useful commentary and investing ideas.

The simplest use of Globeinvestor is to get a snapshot view of the markets or to look up quotes, charts, financial ratios, analyst recommendations and other information for a stock you're interested in. But what separates Globeinvestor from the competition is the content that goes beyond just numbers. News and commentary from *Globe* journalists and outside experts is available, including investing blogs and a feature called Number Cruncher that puts various screening ideas to work in creating lists of stocks and mutual funds for your consideration.

Globeinvestor offers a level of information that will please hardcore investors, but it welcomes novices and intermediates as well by providing tutorials, and explanatory videos.

I'm hardly an unbiased source when it comes to Globeinvestor, so you'll want to verify whether my description of the site is accurate. If you find a better investing site for Canadian investors, I want to hear about it.

2. Yahoo Finance (finance.yahoo.com, ca.finance.yahoo.com)

I really like Yahoo's approach to a financial website—little in the way of visual pizzazz but incredibly easy to use and quite handy. Here's the problem: the U.S. version of Yahoo Finance is easily a hundred times better than the Canadian version.

Let's say you're following a company and you want to see what the financial media have been saying about it. The U.S. version of Yahoo provides links to all kinds of articles on other websites, as well as relevant blog postings. The Canadian version of Yahoo gives you links to standard news releases for a company, and nothing more.

One area where Yahoo excels is in enabling users to track multiple portfolios of stocks. In no time at all, you can name a portfolio, fill it up with a few stocks and decide what information you'd like to keep track of. You won't find any visual pyrotechnics here, just a quick and easy source of key information on stocks you're following.

3. Google Finance (google.com/finance, google.ca/finance)

The mere fact that Google is behind this site suggests there will be clever, user-friendly touches that other sites won't have. In fact, Google Finance is super-easy to use and worth fooling around with for information on Canadian, U.S. and global stocks.

An example of Google's cleverness: recent news stories are synched with stock charts so that you can see how each event or announcement affected the share price. Another example: Google Finance charts make it easy to compare a stock against the appropriate index, and then tell you the percentage gain or loss in a stock over whatever time frame you choose.

Google also does a good job of aggregating coverage of stocks from all kinds of media, including blogs, although once again Canadian stocks don't get the same degree of coverage as U.S. stocks.

4. MarketWatch (marketwatch.com)

This is a U.S. site—it's part of *The Wall Street Journal* Digital Network—and that means zero coverage of Canada on most days. But if you want a U.S. and global perspective on investing or financial markets, you can't do better than MarketWatch.

The focus of MarketWatch is on news rather than investing tools (although some of the tools are pretty good). You get an eclectic mix of market, investing, corporate and political news, all of it written in a brisk, smart style aimed at providing the facts that busy investors need to know about. If news out of the United States or abroad is weighing heavily on global markets, this is an ideal place to get the details.

As for investing tools, there's a cool portfolio tracker on this site that has innovative ways of presenting data in a graphic way instead of just listing numbers. Helpful hint: type "CA:" in front of Canadian stock symbols, as in CA:CRQ.

5. Sedar (sedar.com)

Publicly traded corporations and investment funds must file a steady stream of disclosure documents to securities regulators. Sedar, which stands for System for Electronic Document Analysis and Retrieval, is where investors go to read these filings. Think of Sedar as an essential site for savvy investors who know enough to look beyond the sales pitches when researching mutual funds, closed-end funds, exchange-traded funds and stocks.

Considering a particular mutual fund for your portfolio? For sure, you should check out Globeinvestor.com and Morningstar.ca for useful data and analysis. Then, go to Sedar and download the simplified prospectus for the fund. You'll get an in-depth discussion of the fund's past performance, all relevant fees and commissions, the investment strategies it uses and the risks investors face. Next, download the most recent management report of fund performance, a semi-annual document that is supposed to provide a frank analysis of how the fund has done lately (regulators in the past have criticized fund companies for ducking tough questions in these reports, but that's another story). You also get the most up-to-date information on how much it costs to own the fund, including a historical look back over the previous five years, as well as an update on the fund's top holdings and its asset mix. If you're buying a fund, you should know this stuff before you commit your money.

6. Stockhouse (stockhouse.com)

This Canadian website has been around since the early days of the Internet and has recently evolved into what it describes as a community of investors who share views and questions through discussion forums and blogs. Mining for nuggets of information about a stock you're following? Then Stockhouse is worth visiting.

Start by calling up a quote of your stock. You'll get detailed trading information and a rating of how the stock looks from a technical standpoint (momentum based on price and volume of trading data). Scroll down the page and you'll find a list of mentions of your stock in blog postings on the site. Scroll still further down and you'll find mentions of your stock in Stockhouse's Bullboards, which are online discussion groups.

Stockhouse is all about clever packaging of the thoughts and musings of its community members. There's a Community Pulse feature that shows which stocks are generating the most bull-board activity, and lists of the most read and most commented-upon blogs. There are online discussion forums available on lots of other websites, including TheLion.com, Silicon Investor and Yahoo Finance. But Stockhouse may be the best organized of them all.

7. RiskGrades (riskgrades.com)

Do you look down as well as up when buying a stock? That is, do you consider the possibility of losing money as well as generating profits? If so, what's your tool for assessing risk? You can use the price-earnings ratio, which measures how much a company's stock costs in comparison to how much money it's making, and you can look at historical charts to see how it behaved in bear markets. A worthwhile addition to your risk-assessment toolbox is RiskGrades, a free but very high-tech website created by a firm called RiskMetrics Group.

RiskMetrics, which was spun off years ago from the investment dealer J.P. Morgan, does risk analysis for major investment firms and corporations. On its RiskGrades website, you can apply a surprisingly sophisticated version of these services to your own portfolio. At its simplest, RiskGrades offers a way to get a quick numerical risk score for a stock (the database includes Canadian and global stocks). The score, called a RiskGrade Measure, assesses the level of variation in the price of a stock against the volatility of a basket of global equities. RiskGrade Measures range from zero for cash to as high as 1,000.

At its most elaborate, RiskGrades will assess the risk of your overall stock portfolio and then present the data in chart or graph form. This is simply an outstanding tool for understanding how the individual stocks you own gel overall. RiskGrades is one of the best investment tools available on the Internet and the fact that's its free is amazing.

QuickSurvey: A Comparative Snapshot Look at the Risks Involved in Owning a Selection of a Dozen Canadian Stocks

Company	Ticker (TSX)	RiskGrade Measure
Canadian National Railway	CNR	199
Empire Co.	EMP.A	209
Enbridge	ENB	180
Imperial Oil	IMO	292
Manulife Financial	MFC	333
Potash Corp. of Sask.	POT	557
Research in Motion	RIM	535
RioCan REIT	REI.UN	249
Royal Bank of Canada	RY	269
Teck Cominco	TCK.B	505
Timminco	TIM	535

FIVE MORE WORTHWHILE INVESTING WEBSITES

These sites aren't essentials, but they're well worth bookmarking and visiting on a regular basis.

1. MSN Money (moneycentral.msn.com, finance.sympatico.msn.ca) As it's a Microsoft production, this website offers some of the coolest investing tools around in its Investing zone. For example, StockScouter, which applies a variety of analytical criteria to a stock and then assigns a score out of ten. Another example: Research Wizard, which is like having an expert guide you through a fairly detailed analysis of a stock.

MSN Money has a roster of columnists who are worth reading, a special section for exchange-traded funds and slick tools for charting stocks, among other things. Canadian content? For that, you're best to try Sympatico MSN Finance, which unfortunately is nowhere near as good as MSN Money.

2. Stingy Investor (ndir.com)

This somewhat obscure gem of a website focuses on value investing, which is the quest for beaten-down stocks that offer rebound potential. It's full of articles, suggested stocks and links to other websites and it's a great source of investing ideas.

Stingy Investor has been around since the very early days of online investing. It's maintained by Norman Rothery, a doctor of physics, computer expert and investing professional who, as of the writing of this book, worked as the chief investment strategist for Dan Hallett & Associates, an investment research and financial consulting firm (Dan Hallett is one of Canada's best mutual fund analysts, by the way).

The content on this site includes both investing theory— there's lots of coverage of portfolio building, with an emphasis on costs—and stock picking. Rothery often provides stock suggestions that were selected according to the principles of Benjamin Graham, the father of value investing, and his own "stingy" criteria. Rothery is a prolific writer of articles for publications like *MoneySense* magazine and *Canadian MoneySaver*, and links to many of them are available on the site.

3. TheStreet.com

This is where you'll find the daily musings/rantings of Jim Cramer, the celebrity stock picker and former hedge fund manager. There's a good roster of other columnists on this site, plus solid coverage of day-to-day market happenings. If you're looking for investing ideas, this site is well worth consulting on a regular basis.

4. BigCharts (bigcharts.marketwatch.com)

There are probably dozens of websites where you can produce sophisticated stock charts, but this is one of the first and best. A small added bonus is the historical quotes function, which will show you share prices on any given day going back decades. There's no problem charting Canadian stocks (or getting historical quotes) on this site—just type "CA:" in front of the symbol, as in CA:BCE.

5. Value Investigator (valueinvestigator.com)

This site is maintained by Irwin Michael, one of Canada's best-known value investors. Value investors are the ace bargain hunters of the financial world. Their mission: uncover sound stocks that are temporarily trading at discounted prices and try to profit off a recovery. Michael struggled in the bear market, but he has made solid returns for his high-net-worth clientele over the long term. If you want to know which stocks Michael is buying, try this website. You will find Michael's original rationale for buying the stock, as well as periodic updates. Michael also gives word when he sells a holding.

FIVE BLOGS THAT WILL MAKE YOU A SMARTER INVESTOR

Blogs are an unbelievably good source of information for investors, which may come as a surprise to you given that blogs tend to be written by financial amateurs—in other words, people in work in other professions and regard investing as a hobby or avocation. But from my experience, there tends to be a high level of accuracy and common-sense utility from many investing blogs. Here are some of the best examples.

1. Canadian Capitalist (canadiancapitalist.com)

If you only have time to read one investing blog, make it this one. It's maintained by an Ottawa software developer named Ram Balakrishnan who has been blogging since late 2004 and really knows his stuff. The analysis here is not only sound, it's smart. As a good blog should, Canadian Capitalist produces a steady flow of original material supplemented by periodic listings of interesting posts from other blogs.

2. The Dividend Guy (thedividendguyblog.com)

The recession that took hold in 2008 was so vicious that even some stalwart dividend-paying companies had to trim their quarterly payouts to investors—or suspend them altogether. As I write this, Dow Chemical had just cut its dividend for the first time since it began paying them in 1912. This is a roundabout way of saying that if you're interested in dividend investing—and you should be if you have any sense—you need a good source of guidance to help you pick the best possible dividend stocks. The Dividend Guy's your guy in this regard.

3. Where Does All My Money Go (wheredoesallmymoneygo.com)

This blog is written by Preet Banerjee, a former financial adviser, and it's full of practical ruminations on matters like how much of a registered education savings plan should go into fixed income (bonds and GICs, in other words) and where to find a fee-only financial planner. Watch for Banerjee's weekly roundup of interesting posts on other investing blogs.

4. Larry MacDonald (blog.canadianbusiness.com/category/larry-macdonald/)

MacDonald is a former economist who now blogs for the *Canadian Business* website on investing matters. What distinguishes this blog from most others is that it's closely tied to current events in the financial world, including new product launches. MacDonald does a particularly good job of keeping on top of developments in the world of exchange-traded funds, which are a favourite of many investing bloggers.

5. Steadyhand (steadyhand.com)

This blog is different from the four above in that it's produced by people who are active in the investing industry. Steadyhand is a small, relatively new mutual fund company run by Tom Bradley, former head of Phillips, Hager & North. You most certainly do not get the standard Bay Street view from Bradley and his cohorts. They're quick to point out the failings of the fund industry while also looking at practical investing matters and stocks of interest. Call this blog an antidote to sales-oriented propaganda produced by the investment industry.

THREE INVESTING NEWSLETTERS WORTH YOUR TIME AND MONEY

What you must understand about investing newsletters and pay websites is that they're a business, first and foremost. They need to attract subscribers to make money, so they often make claims about their stock-picking prowess that can sound unbelievable. Here are some newsletters that I've followed for years and believe to be solid (though not infallible) sources of investing ideas.

1. *The Investment Reporter*

If you're new to investing in stocks and see yourself as a buy-and-hold investor focusing on quality, and not a speculator or active trader, you can't do much better than this fixture of the Canadian investment newsletter scene. *The Investment Reporter* was founded in 1941 and still appears each week with lists of recommended stocks.

This newsletter is clear, concise and as jargon-free as it could realistically be, given its focus on a subject that can get technical at times. Expect an emphasis on large, blue-chip dividend-paying stocks, as opposed to the smaller companies that sometimes make the news because of their meteoric share price gains. But that doesn't mean *The Investment Reporter*'s recommendations are laggards. The *Hulbert Financial Digest,* a U.S. publication that tracks North American investment newsletters, has found that *The Investment Reporter*'s picks gained 13.8 per cent annually on average for the twenty years ending December 31, 2007—a track record that beat the S&P/TSX composite index and Canadian equity mutual funds as well.

Because it appears weekly, *The Investment Reporter* can be expensive to subscribe to at a rate of $327 annually (a $97 introductory rate has been offered in the past). However, this newsletter is also available in libraries. There's also an online version available at investmentreporter.com.

QuickProfile

Details: By mail on a weekly basis

Web: investmentreporter.com

Phone: 1-800-804-8846 or 416-869-1177

Cost: $57 intro rate for six months, $327 per year regular rate

2. The Successful Investor

This newsletter operates on much the level as *The Investment Reporter*, which means it aims to be a source of stock ideas for investors who want to build a well-rounded long-term portfolio. The editor is Patrick McKeough, a one-time stockbroker who oversaw *The Investment Reporter* before moving on to set up his own stable of newsletters.

I've been reading *The Successful Investor* for years and have often noted how McKeough seems at times to be out of step with what brokerage analysts and other market watchers are saying. My money's on McKeough in these cases. He has a level-headed, seen-it-all way of analyzing stocks that really seems to both make sense and achieve good results on the whole.

More aggressive investors might want to check out *Stock Picker's Digest*, a sister publication designed for speculative investors, while conservative types should consider *Canadian Wealth Advisor*. Each serves its niche well and can be considered a reliable source of investing ideas.

QuickProfile

Details: By mail on a monthly basis

Web: thesuccessfulinvestor.com

Phone: 1–800–579–4246 or 416–756–0397

Cost: $72 per year

3. *Internet Wealth Builder*

This newsletter is edited by Gordon Pape, who pretty much pioneered investing and personal-finance writing for everyday people in this country. *Internet Wealth Builder* is the most widely appealing of Pape's newsletters and, in one way, it stands out above all others: accountability. No one revisits past picks and frankly assesses how they've worked out like Pape. When a pick turns out to be a dud, he admits it and tells readers to sell. By the way, there's no shame in this. Anyone who claims to bat anything close to 1.000 as a stock picker is a liar.

Pape gets regular contributions from various outside experts for the *Internet Wealth Builder,* and together they provide a steady flow of investing ideas that include both Canadian and U.S. stocks, blue-chips as well as somewhat more speculative names. Subscriber questions are also answered on a regular basis.

A related newsletter is *The Income Investor,* which specializes in the vast slice of the public whose primary investment goal is to generate income. There's also *Mutual Funds Update,* which focuses on funds. Whichever you choose, you get one of the country's top investing commentators working for you.

QuickProfile

Details: By email 44 times per year

Web: buildingwealth.ca

Phone: 1-888-287-8229 or 416-693-8526

Cost: $144.95 per year

THE SUREFIRE WAY TO TELL IF AN INVESTING NEWSLETTER OR PAY WEBSITE IS JUNK

The Internet has given new life to investing newsletters and stock-picking services that claim to have the markets figured out. The usual pitch: market-beating advice on what stocks to buy. The usual reality: a complete waste of money for subscribers. Here's what to look for so you avoid these traps.

Extravagant, Boastful Claims about Investment Returns

An email I got not too long ago flogged a website selling investment advice that included the name of a "fund"—that was as specific as things got—with a track record of paying an average dividend of 24.9 per cent annually over the previous five years. Maybe such a fund exists. But the chances of you buying it and reaping that return over the next five years are about the same as the Toronto Maple Leafs winning the Stanley Cup in each of those years. Okay, maybe the chances of the former are a little better than the latter. But you get the point: 24.9 per cent is a crazily extravagant yield for any sort of legitimate stock or fund.

Three, four, maybe five per cent—those sound like results based in reality. Any higher than that and you have to take the yield as a warning sign. Remember: yields measure the percentage return a dividend or interest payment gives you on the amount of money you invested upfront. A rising yield tells you that the price of a stock, fund or bond is falling, and that's a bad sign. A 24.9-per-cent yield? That's bad like the inaugural voyage of the *Titanic* was bad.

Smart investing newsletters stand on the credentials of their writers, the authority of their analysis and the track record of their selections. They don't use overheated prose that implies they're doing something that no other mortal investors can do.

Be particularly wary of claims about beating the market, which means returns that exceed what the appropriate benchmark stock index made. For one thing, very few stock pickers beat the index on a consistent basis (getting lucky for a year or two is not out of the question). For another, it's extremely difficult to verify market-beating claims, even when you're presented with a chart full of data. Let's say a newsletter presents data showing a portfolio of its picks beat the index over a period of time. Are the newsletter's duds included there? Is there documentation of exactly when the stocks were recommended, and what the percentage gain or loss was until the newsletter was published? These are questions you'll want to ask before paying for your subscription. If you can't get the answers, that's an answer in itself.

FIVE WAYS TO VERIFY A NEWSLETTER'S BONA FIDES

You've no doubt heard of the principle of being innocent until proven guilty? Well, investing newsletters are a waste of money unless proven useful. Here are some ways to make sure you're buying the real goods in a newsletter.

1. It offers you a free trial copy.

This seems basic. How can you be expected to pay a significant sum—many newsletters cost $100 to $300 a year or more—for a publication you can't sample in advance?

2. The background of the author(s) is documented.

If you're buying investment advice from someone, you want to know all about them. Don't settle for a canned bio. As well, do a Google search to see where this person's name crops up. Are they quoted by serious financial journalists? Have they written books? Have they worked at name-brand Bay Street or Wall Street firms? Remember that anyone can put together a zippy website. Real credibility is much rarer.

3. The investing style is clearly explained.

The best investing newsletters have a specialty, be it speculative investing, blue-chips or dividends and income. You should be able to tell exactly what kind of recommendations you'll get, and what strategies and rationales were used to select them.

4. Penny stocks aren't the focus.

There's a whole sub-genre of investing newsletters and websites devoted to speculative stocks priced at less than a dollar or two, particularly those in the mining and energy fields. If this is your area of interest, shop carefully. If you're more of a generalist, take a pass on this type of newsletter. Big scores can certainly be had by speculating in penny stocks, but this type of investing is basically a form of gambling.

5. The newsletter is endorsed by other investors.

Ask your investing friends, contacts and relatives what newsletters they've found useful, and also which ones they've subscribed to and cancelled due to general uselessness.

THREE VERY USEFUL INVESTING CALCULATORS

Some of the most useful online applications in terms of investment planning are calculators that do the number-crunching for you. Here are a few especially good examples.

1. Ativa Interactive (ativa.com)

This company is in the business of designing financial software for the investment industry and it offers a great selection of calculators available for free on its website. There's an inventive, topical quality to the calculators on this site that you don't see elsewhere. For example, Ativa had calculators focused on tax-free savings accounts as soon as they became available in early 2009. At the same time, it offered several options for helping investors make sense of what the bear market for stocks meant to their portfolios.

2. Fiscal Agents (fiscalagents.com)

This website for this financial planning firm has a "financial tools" area with a huge collection of online calculators that cover personal finance stuff like mortgages and debt as well as retirement and investment planning. A great collection.

3. Compound Interest Calculator (1728.com/compint.htm.)

A simple but highly useful calculator that allows you to quickly see how much an investment might grow at various rates of return. You can play around with the variables here, which means it's possible to specify how much money you started with and how much you have now, then figure out your rate of return.

INDEX